THE COUNTRY RHYMES OF
JAMES ORR

THE BARD OF BALLYCARRY
1770 - 1816

THE FOLK POETS OF ULSTER

TITLES IN THE SERIES

VOLUME ONE
THE COUNTRY RHYMES OF
HUGH PORTER
THE BARD OF MONEYSLANE

VOLUME TWO
THE COUNTRY RHYMES OF
JAMES ORR
THE BARD OF BALLYCARRY

VOLUME THREE
THE COUNTRY RHYMES OF
SAMUEL THOMSON
THE BARD OF CARNGRANNY

PRETANI PRESS

THE COUNTRY RHYMES OF

JAMES ORR

THE BARD OF BALLYCARRY

1770 - 1816

WITH AN INTRODUCTION BY

PHILIP ROBINSON

First published by Pretani Press, 1992
78 Abbey Street, Bangor BT20 4JB

Introduction copyright ©
Philip Robinson

This book has received financial assistance under
the Cultural Traditions Programme which aims to
encourage acceptance and understanding of
cultural diversity.

Design and typesetting by Pegasus Design Consultants, Belfast.
Photography by Gemini, Belfast.
Antiques supplied by Robert Huffam, Carrickfergus.
Original maps by Alison Hogg.
Printed in Northern Ireland by
W. & G. Baird Ltd.

ISBN 0 948868 17 1

PRETANI PRESS

CONTENTS

THE FOLK POETS OF ULSTER

The vernacular poetical tradition in Ulster was part of a much broader literary movement focussed in Scotland and culminating in the work of Robert Burns at the end of the eighteenth century. This virile Ulster tradition, much of it written in lowland Scots, has its beginnings early in the eighteenth century, before the work of Burns.

The works produced by the writers in this tradition were rescued by the late John Hewitt, in his book *Rhyming Weavers* (first published in 1974). This caused the value of these poets to be recognised by local historians, giving as they do a peasant's eye view of local life and customs, attitudes to religion and politics and such matters.

The purpose of this series is not to interpret or explain the poems, but to make them accessible once more, and to provide for each poet a biographical sketch. Some, nearly all, of the original volumes are extremely rare, and only found in the larger scholarly libraries.

Where the poets were prolific and produced several volumes, a selection has been made which prefers those written in Ulster-Scots rather than standard English, and which cover themes of local and historical interest.

The main era of publication was from c.1790 to c.1840, in the immediate wake of Burns' first edition of 1786, and during this period dozens of Ulster poets (notably from the counties of Down and Antrim) produced volumes of verse, mainly supported by subscriptions (pre-publication orders), overwhelmingly from friends and neighbours.

The vigorous Ulster-Scots of these poets will be difficult reading for even fluent speakers of modern vernacular. It is recommended that in reading those poems the full depth of meaning will not be transmitted unless a dialect dictionary (e.g. *The Concise Scots Dictionary*) is used frequently - even for those words which look familiar.

Series Editors:
J. R. R. Adams
P. S. Robinson

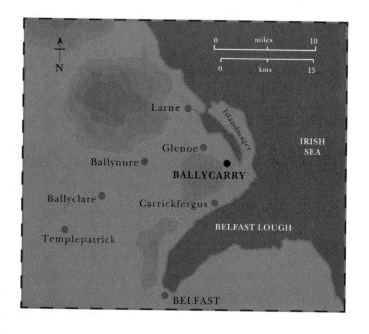

INTRODUCTION

James Orr is widely acclaimed as the best of the Ulster folk
poets, of which there were a great number even in his own
generation. Almost two centuries after his first poems were
published, Orr remains the best-known, the most studied,
and the most popular of all. In many ways he provides us
with the stereotype of the Ulster weaver-poet of the 1790s
and early 1800s - a radical thinker, a patriot, a United
Irishman, a 'New Light' Presbyterian, a humanist with a
penetrating social concern for the poor, a contented
weaver and small farmer who never sought social elevation,
and a man who until his death in 1817 continued to speak
'braid Scotch'. The late John Hewitt, in *Rhyming Weavers*
(his impressive study of the folk poets published in 1974),
described some of Orr's poems as being far beyond the
capacity of any of our other rural rhymers. Two of these
poems, 'The Penitent' and 'The Irish Cottier's Death and
Burial', he described as 'undoubtedly the major successes
in scale in our vernacular literature'. When Orr wrote in
Scots he displayed his considerable literary skill to greatest
effect. However Hewitt described his English verses as only
'competent, but seldom more than that'. As far as the
poem 'The Irish Cottier's Death and Burial' was
concerned, several modern writers (Hewitt included) have
offered the opinion that this was perhaps even better
written than Robert Burns' equivalent in 'The Cotter's
Saturday Night'.

James Orr was born in 1770 in a thatched, single storey
house, about a mile west of the village of Ballycarry in east
Antrim. His father, also called James Orr, was a weaver with
a few acres of land taken on lease from the Red Hall Estate,
then owned by R Gervas Ker Esq. In this small house James
Orr was taught by his father to weave linen on a hand-loom
and to read and write. He had a second cousin, Thomas
Beggs, another well-known folk poet born in Glenwhirry in
1789, who described Orr as 'the Shakespeare of the
plebeian train'. As with most of the folk poets (and with
most of Orr's relatives), his circumstances were poor in
material things. Orr's parents were also extremely

protective of their only child. It is not clear if their concern was for his morals, or for his delicate health, but in fact he was never allowed to attend school. Having learnt to read and write from his father at home, he began attending singing classes as a young boy in the Ballycarry Presbyterian Meeting-House. Here he made his first attempts at poetry as the young boys and girls competed with each other to compose secular rhymes for the well-known Psalm tunes of the day. This was common practice in Presbyterian communities because the words of the Psalms themselves were only to be sung in worship. Orr's compositions were outstandingly better than his contemporaries, but such doggerel poems were common currency at the time. 'Crambo' verses were much the same, crambo being a popular parlour game involving the composition of a single line, which then had to be answered by another person in rhyme as quickly and as originally as possible. In a self-effacing way, many of the folk-poets described their own efforts as 'crambo', and indeed the Templepatrick bard, Samuel Thomson, even called his house 'Crambo Cave'.

Almost 50 poems of local and dialect interest written by James Orr have been selected for this volume, but these represent less than one-third of the total he is known to have published. The selection has not been made on literary grounds, although if we accept that Orr's poems in Scots are indeed his best, then virtually all of these have been included. The remainder of the present selection written in English have been chosen because they provide some descriptive content of local historic or social interest, along with a few other poems that help us understand the man himself better. The omitted items, despite being all written in English and of marginal local interest, are not necessarily poorer poems for that. Indeed some of the omitted poems are important ones dealing with international issues and major historic events such as the 'Soliloquy of Bonaparte' and 'The ruin of Moscow'.

Returning to Orr's early life, he had been born late in his parents' marriage. As far as can be judged, neither his father nor his mother shared his radical turn of mind, for they appeared to have been 'Auld Licht' and rather conservative in their Calvinistic theology. In all probability they also disapproved of his participation in the '98 rebellion. It has been suggested that Orr's father educated him at home to shelter him from the prevailing radical thought that characterised the 'Enlightenment' in Scotland and east Ulster. If this was the case it was a singularly unsuccessful schooling, at least in that respect. Orr's attitude to the restrictive views of his own parents was bitterly expressed in the poem 'A parents Flinty Heart'. In this poem the poet waked from his sleep to lament that his parents' hard hearts could never learn 'To rule, yet spare. To shield and not enslave'. Indeed it becomes clear that Orr left home for America after participating in the 1798 rebellion, not simply because he was forced to flee from the Authorities, but after being rejected by his parents' 'flinty hearts'.

> 'The more you mark'd my passive mind,
>   The more you tyraniz'd;
> As from your door, in woe and wail,
>   You drove me - both to part.
> You pray'd that grace might guide. What cant
>   Incrusts a flinty heart'.

In another poem 'The Glen', which was written about the natural beauty of a childhood haunt (Old Mill glen in the Red Hall demesne) he wrote:

> 'Should tyranny spurn thee from home,
>   The Glen thou shalt live in with me'.

Orr added a footnote here to the word tyranny to explain it as 'meaning parental authority', lest the landlord (R Gervas Ker, Esq) should think he was alluding to anything else.

Orr's relationship with his parents was complex, and their formative influence on him cannot be easily summarised or disentangled. His father died shortly after his return from a short stay in America in 1799, and some time before 1804 when he published his first book of poems. In the 1804 volume he included an 'Epitaph for the Author's Father' which is warm and loving, and no less so than the 'Lament for a beloved and affectionate Mother' included in the second volume of posthumous works published in 1817.

It was probably during the spring of 1799 that Orr stayed in America for a few months. He appears as 'James Orr, Jun.' in the list of subscribers to Samuel Thomson's 1793 volume of poetry (Thomson was the first Ulster folk poet to have a collected volume of his own poems published), but not in the list for Thomson's second volume of 1799. Local tradition states that Orr left immediately following the '98 rebellion, but only remained in America a few months. We know that he had returned promptly, for he applied to join the local Yeomanry in 1800 in response to the perceived Napoleonic threat. Apart from the internal evidence of his own 1804 volume of poems, (the 'Penitent' was written in 1800), he appears in the list of subscribers to Hugh Tynan of Donaghadee's volume of poems which was printed in 1803.

The earliest published poems of James Orr are to be found under a fictitious name in the *Northern Star*, the journal of the United Irishmen which had been founded in Belfast in 1792, a year after the Society itself had been formed. None of these were subsequently republished, but it is probable that two poems appearing under the name 'A Patriot' were by Orr. These were 'The Tears of Liberty' (*Northern Star*, November 4, 1796) and 'Virtue's Polar Star' (*Northern Star*, March 6, 1797). Of course many of Orr's poems did relate to the 1798 United Irishmen's rising in which he took part, but these were clearly written after the event. They were published in his first volume *Poems on various subjects* which appeared in 1804. Orr seems always to have regarded the pen as mightier than the sword, although he briefly succumbed to the temptation of the latter in '98. One of the poems published in the 1804 volume was entitled 'A Prayer, written on the eve of the unfortunate 7th of June, 1798', which at least demonstrates that he continued to write poetry throughout those troubled times. Whether from parental or governmental 'tyranny', he left Larne for America shortly after the rebellion. Although only there for a few months, Orr did publish some poetry for the American press. The editor of an American newspaper added his own prefix to one poem: 'We understand the present production is by James Orr, an humble weaver from the North of Ireland. We could wish that his writings were better known'.

It is interesting to speculate as to how Orr stood as a poet among his contemporaries. His only serious rival to being the most celebrated rural bard of his day was Samuel Thomson of Lyles Hill, near Templepatrick. Thomson had the advantage of a better formal education and had travelled to Ayrshire to meet Burns in 1794. Indeed he was a schoolmaster with considerable pretensions to classical scholarship. Thomson was the first Ulster poet to publish his own volume (in 1793), and also managed a second in 1799 before Orr achieved the publication of his own volume. Thomson and Orr were on friendly terms, but they kept a certain formality in their relationship. Thomson was less consistently radical than Orr in his politics, and although he employed the Scots tongue with good effect in his early poems, he was also a conservative in his Presbyterianism. The following abstracts of an undated letter from Orr to Thompson are interesting, for they show that Orr was not intimidated by Thomson's education, his literary standing or his new-found pro-Establishment thinking.

Mr S Thompson
Crambo Cave

Dear Sir,

You want to know my opinion of your last publication and l shall candidly give it. The epistle to Lamont, as published in the Microscope was excellent, but you have added some stanzas which have somewhat impaired its beauty ... Of the Gloaming you already know my opinion ...

Your address to the Rising is far superior to the one to the Setting Sun and were it not for a tincture of Calvanistic Divinity that

......es some of the verses displeasing to my Taste, I'd call it the best in the Miscellany.

... And now permit me to mention a few that I would rather you had suppressed ...

... Concerning the books, I have not as yet the price of them all, but that will be no loss to you. I seldom see or hear Mr Paul, but as I understand he holds his sacrament in Carnmony, I will (if health permit) call at Crambo Cave on the Saturday before it, and punctually pay you.

Yours fraternally
          James Orr

This letter was written *circa* 1806, and shows how quickly Orr's confidence had grown in a few years. Thomson was virtually the 'Bard in Residence' for the *Northern Star* with regular contributions, and quickly adapted his stance to make his poetry acceptable for the *Belfast News-letter* after 1798. In 1802 Orr's first poem appears in the *News-letter*. This was his 'Verses on the Death of Hugh Tynan', and a note was added:

'*Our Readers will no doubt, be inclined to pardon any inaccuracies in the above Poem, when they are informed, that this is the production of a humble tradesman, who was never a day at school, nor had he ever the assistance of a tutor of any kind (save what little instruction his father was enabled to give him) and who is now about the same age that TYNAN was when he died'.*

The physical appearance of James Orr was that of a man of 'stature rather low, but well formed; his cheeks were ruddy and his eyes expressive and lively'. James Fullerton in the *Ulster Magazine* of May 1801 described him as a man 'of middle stature, slightly stooped, with hair a pale chestnut colour. His voice was slow and he spoke broad Scotch till his death'. A story was told locally that when James Orr's poems were being printed, he walked one morning from Ballycarry to Belfast to examine the proof sheets of his works. One of the young men in the office failed to recognise him and took him to be a rustic fool. He asked Orr if he had seen the men whitewashing the Cavehill as he came into town - to which Orr is said to have replied (in verse that he would probably have disowned).

> To whitewash the Cavehill
> Tis what they ne'er will
> But <u>Time</u> may its rough garb renew
> With sweet growing showers
> To moisten its flowers
> And wither such cockscombs as you.

When Orr died on 24 April 1816, the *Belfast Literary Journal* noted in its obituary of the 'self-taught rural bard' that he was known as exceptionally 'warm, generous, and social-hearted'. Shortly before his death, Orr requested a few friends to arrange the unpublished poems he had composed since his 1804 volume, and prepare them for the press. The profits were to be distributed among the poor of the parish of Broadisland, his native place. *The Posthumous Works of James Orr of Ballycarry*, was published in 1817 in Belfast by a close friend, A M'Dowell of Ballycarry, who also included a 'Sketch of the Author's Life'. In this sketch the portrait of a kind, generous and sociable man is painted - somewhat unnecessarily, for the personal qualities of Orr shine so brightly through his own poems. His moderate temperament can be seen even in the introduction he wrote for the 1804 volume: 'I have one consolation, that if my production should offend the taste, they will not corrupt the morals; sorry would I be if they contained a single line that could ferment party spirit or alarm the devout heart'. His last years were spent in poor health, in the same thatched house he had been born in 46 years before. M'Dowell tells us that 'he often fled the cheerless habitation of the bachelor, and was obliged to seek the pleasures of society at an inn'.

Many of Orr's later poems and songs were composed for performing at the festive boards of Masonic Lodges, or at other gatherings such as the Soiree held by the Moravian congregation at Gracehill. Orr seemed to have been spurred on by a genuine love of unsophisticated friendship, and a need for the fellowship and acclaim of common folk. His friend and biographer A M'Dowell, concluded that this led to his downfall. His only intemperance was at the inn, and these 'errors of his latter years' could not detract from his achievements: 'whatever might be his defects, candour and openness of mind, a generous and feeling heart never once forsook him. His honesty and integrity were unquestioned; and he retained to the last a manly and independent spirit'.

Orr was buried in Templecorran graveyard in Ballycarry in 1816, and in 1831 an imposing monument was erected on his grave, paid for by Masonic subscription. The foundation stone of this monument was laid at a ceremony attended by members of the Masonic Order in full regalia, and the monument itself has classical detailing covered with masonic symbols. It contains a number of inscriptions, not least of which is a 12-verse poetic 'Elegy' by A M'Dowell (which appears in even longer form as a prefix to M'Dowell's 1817 edition of Orr's *Posthumous Works*). The only verses of Orr's own on the monument are the lines:

> *'When lost among nettles, ye'll find if ye search*
> *My stone o' remembrance is marked wi' an arch'.*

The esteem in which he was later regarded is proclaimed on one face:

> *"This monument to the Poet, the Patriot and the*
> *Philanthropist was erected by the contributions of*
> *various liberal individuals in Broadisland,*
> *Carrickfergus, Isle Magee, Larne, Belfast,*
> *Ballymena, and of the following Masonic Lodges,*
> *viz the Grand Lodge of Ireland and Nos 41,*
> *43,107,162, 175,177, 256, 248, 253, 615,1012,*
> *and 1014, Orr's own Lodge, encouraged by the*
> *General Muse of his Brethren M'KENZIE, BEGGS*

> *and ENGLISH: ... The first stone was laid by*
> *the Rev W Glendy on the 21st June 1831 in*
> *presence of the assembled Brethren. "*

One of these 'Brother Bards' of Orr's (James Russell
English) published a poem in 1830 called 'The Late James
Orr', which is virtually an appeal for subscriptions to raise
the monument. English wrote a note to this poem as
follows:

> *'So lightly has Irish genius been estimated, that*
> *JAMES ORR, though styled by contemporary writers*
> *the 'Burns of Ulster', has reposed in a nameless*
> *grave in the Churchyard of Templecorran, for 14*
> *years. Since writing the above lines, however, it is*
> *understood that a few patriotic individuals have*
> *set foot a subscription for the pupose of erecting a*
> *monument over the grave of Ulster's Rural Bard'.*

James Orr's attitudes to religion have been studied by
Linde Connolly Lunney and these were published in *Ulster
Folklife* Vol 31, 1985. This article examined Orr's attitudes
to life and death based on the internal evidence of his
poetry, and the author argues convincingly that Orr
himself favoured the New Light theology which we would
today identify as being acceptable only to Non-Subscribing
Presbyterians. A generation later Deism, Unitarianism, and
Arianism (where the divinity of Christ as an integral part of
the Trinity was questioned) were to become regarded as
'official' heresies by the orthodox Presbyterian Church, but
were matters of individual choice within the
Presbyterianism of Orr's day. The schism within
Presbyterianism which resulted in most of the Unitarian
and Arian adherents leaving to form their own Synod as
Remonstrant (later 'Non-Subscribing') Presbyterians only
crystallised in the 1820s. During Orr's time the debate
raged within congregations, and not between
denominations, and this fact is reflected in Orr's own
slightly ambivalent attitude. He was by nature disinclined
towards any heated dispute that might cause offence. He

ned flexible and open-minded even towards ᵈᵒₓ Calvinism and towards his friends that reacted conservatively to what they saw as 'New Licht' excesses. It is probable that his parents were of the 'Auld Licht' school, and after their death Orr may have been less inclined to rebel against their rigidity. Certainly he wrote an 'Ode to the Rev Henry Cooke, Donegore' in praise of his work in establishing a House of Industry for the poor in Belfast. Cooke of course was to become the arch-enemy of Arianism in Ulster, and Orr established several other friendships with people of like mind to Cooke, including the Covenanting Minister at Lough Mourne: Rev John Paul. He was even to subscribe in 1803 to a posthumous volume of poems by Hugh Tynan of Donaghadee. Tynan's poems were exceptionally conservative and religiously pious, but nevertheless Orr composed a sympathetic elegy to him. If we judge the man by the company he kept, it should be noted that among the lists of subscribers to Orr's 1804 volume appear the names of five Presbyterian clergymen. Three of these were from local congregations: Rev J Murphy of Islandmagee (ordained 1789), Rev Adam Hill of Ballynure (installed 1785), and Orr's own minister at Ballycarry, Rev John Bankhead who was ordained there in 1763. Another two, although they were from more distant congregations, shared Orr's own preference for 'New Light' theology. Rev N Alexander of Crumlin (ordained in 1799) was a licentiate of the Antrim Non-Subscribing Presbytery. He became Moderator of the Synod of Ulster in 1817-1818, but in 1830 he withdrew his congregation from the Synod to joint the Remonstrants. Rev J Watts of Greyabbey, ordained in 1799 after the execution there of Rev James Porter as a suspected United Irishman in 1798, also withdrew his congregation in 1829 from the Synod of Ulster to join the Remonstrants.

One of Orr's finest poems 'The Penitent' was 'inscribed to the Rev J Bankhead, written in the year 1800', and is almost Wesleyan in tone. In some senses this poem was a self-commentary. It tells of the downfall and redemption of a drunken weaver. Orr himself died a lonely victim of drink.

He wrote a number of other poems addressed to Presbyterian ministers he favoured because of their social concern. In particular it is worth noting his 'Address to Rev William Glendy'. Glendy succeeded Bankhead as the Minister at Ballycarry in 1812, and in 1828 he declared himself to be an Arian, taking part of his congregation to the breakaway Remonstrant Synod where Unitarian principles dominated. Glendy was of course the minister who laid the foundation stone for Orr's monument at the Masonic ceremony in Templecorran graveyard in 1831. Orr was only 26 when Burns died in 1796, but an indirect link is provided by the poem 'Elegy on the death of Hugh Blair D.D.' Blair was Professor of Rhetoric at Edinburgh University, and one of the most distinguished Edinburgh Literati of the late 18th century. After Burns' collected poems were published in 1786, Blair took a particular interest in promoting him in Edinburgh society. Indeed they corresponded warmly with each other, probably as a reflection of Blair's own well known 'Moderate-Party' views on religion and politics in Scotland. In 1800 Rev Dr Hugh Blair died, so that it must have been shortly before this that Orr heard what was a prophetic farewell sermon:

> *While fond to hear the far-fam'd foe of vice,*
> *Amidst his audience pensively I lean'd*
> *Sedate I saw him in the rostrum rise*
> *And heard him say with majesty unfeign'd -*
>
> *You I shall teach no more. The prize I reach*
> *But lest you'd wander when my voice should cease,*
> *I've wrote my precepts that they still may teach*
> *An age to come, to follow truth and peace.*

We cannot be sure that Blair did not come to Antrim or Belfast, but it is more likely that Orr travelled to Edinburgh to hear him speak. Again we see the attraction Orr felt for any intelligent debate - whether Covenanter or Unitarian. However the debate for Orr was always within the radical Presbyterian and anti-authoritarian limits of his own experience and commitment.

At the other end of the Presbyterian spectrum were the Reformed Presbyterians, or Covenanters. These were Calvinistic and their nickname of 'Mountain Men' is a reflection of how they were formerly persecuted in Scotland and Ulster during the seventeenth century when they were only able to worship in secret in mountain glens. The nickname also reflects how, within Ulster Presbyterianism of the early 1800s, they were still stigmatised as backward by the New Light intellectuals. The nearest Covenanting congregation to Ballycarry was that of Rev John Paul at Loughmourne - in the upland moors north of Carrickfergus. Paul was no intellectual backwoodsman however, and gained a reputation as the Covenanters' most articulate opponent of Arianism. Orr, always attracted by the cutting edge of intellectual debate, sometimes took the short (less than three miles) journey to Loughmourne, and even travelled to Carnmoney to hear him when Paul opened a second Meeting-House there.

In no way could Orr be regarded as holding eccentric religious or political attitudes within his own community. He was a reflection, indeed it could be said he was a representative, of his time and place. The Parish of Broadisland, centred on Ballycarry, had the earliest Presbyterian congregation in Ireland, dating from 1611 when Sir William Edmonstone of Red Hall brought over Rev Edward Brice, the first Presbyterian minister to come from Scotland to Ireland. Brice is buried alongside Orr in Templecorran graveyard, and incidentally in the same place are the graves of a number of noted United Irishmen, including Nelson, the 'Ballycarry Martyr'.

The influence of the Scottish Enlightenment which is reflected in Orr's poetry was also to be found in the Freemasonry of his day. In the late 1700s Freemasonry and radical politics went hand in hand in east Ulster, often with common membership between local lodges and local corps of United Irishmen. It was probably more because of a search for universal harmony rather than the direct influence of Unitarian principles that Freemasonry began to adopt a more generally Deist approach at this time. However there is no clear distinction in Orr's poems (and probably not in his own attitudes) between his Freemasonry, his enlightened Presbyterian religion, and his patriotic nationalism. His poems on any of these themes often make reference to his other attitudes as well.

After the disaster of the failed '98 rebellion, Orr seems to have quickly reconciled himself to poetry as a means of expressing his radical politics. His concern for international issues also continued, remembering that the United Irishmen had been inspired by events in America and France in the first place. His reaction on the ground to the futility of the rising in which he participated is expressed vividly in the poem 'Donegore Hill'. It is believed that Orr intervened to prevent some of the other east Antrim men 'out' in 1798 from committing atrocities, and that this stood him in good stead in the following years. His reputation as a fair and just man however was not enough to see his application to join the Ballycarry Yeomanry in 1800 accepted. Once again in response to international issues (in this case the Napoleonic threat), Orr had to resort to the pen as the most effective tool of influence for his considerable intellect. It has been said that in 1798 Orr learnt the 'immorality of violence'. It seems equally possible that he realised the hopeless futility of it. Many of his poems reveal a dread of the assizes, the jails and the gallows, and it is most likely he witnessed United Irishmen hangings in Carrickfergus. The most notable such hanging was that of William Orr of Antrim - a namesake of James (but no relation) who provided his compatriots with the cry 'Remember Orr' in 1798.

One theme that runs through many of Orr's poems is his social concern for the poor. In 'The Bull-beat' he extends this concern to man's cruelty to animals in the name of sport, and obviously this concern is not placed in a different category from his religion: 'Can Christians pride in gore and strife?' A similar theme exists in 'To a Sparrow, on seeing some boys rob her Nest'. His concern for the poor and destitute is a recurring theme. In 'The Poor-house - an Elegy', 'The Mendicant's Farewell to his Benefactors - respectfully inserted to the Society for the employment and relief of the poor in the Town of Belfast', and in his 'Ode To The Rev Henry Cooke, Donegore, on his sermon preached for the benefit of the House of Industry, Belfast' we see Orr's passionate interest in the fate of the weak, vulnerable and exploited. It almost seems from the content of these poems that Orr had some inside knowledge of the Poor-House. However the income from his writing probably kept him from abject poverty during his last years of ill-health. It is characteristic of his social concern that he had organised his own *Posthumous works* to be published for the benefit of the poor in Broadisland.

Not all Orr's poems were concerned with mortality or such serious aspects of life. His works provide rich information about the social customs and traditions of every-day living in his community, and many lighthearted works intended to entertain rather than educate include his 'Address to Beer', 'To the Potatoe', 'Tea', 'The Wanderer' and 'The Spae-Wife'. The value of his poetry as a source for local and social history has been demonstrated in the study published in 1977 by D H Akenson and W H Crawford: *Local Poets and Social History: James Orr. Bard of Ballycarry.* Besides providing us with numerous insights into the social life of Orr's day, this study contains selected poems on various themes set beside contemporary documents. For example, the theme of emigration is covered by providing Orr's poem 'The Passengers' (which vividly portrays his own experiences on his voyage to America), alongside an extract of a contemporary document: 'A Journal of a Voyage from Belfast to Boston'. A Poem such as 'The Irish Cottier's Death and Burial' is not only a rich source of social history, but also illustrates local folk customs associated with the 'wake'. Further, it reveals much of Orr's concern for the poor, his religious views on death and mortality, and of course (like all his poems in Scots) is of particular interest to the student of the Ulster-Scots tongue. The late Professor John Braidwood of the Department of English at Queen's University Belfast, an outstanding scholar of the Scots language in Ulster, stated in his inaugural lecture that James Orr '... could, in his "Irish Cottier's Death and Burial", write a poem more securely and consistently Scots than Burns's 'The Cotter's Saturday Night ...' In that same poem, Orr describes how the mourners make an attempt 'to quat braid Scotch, a task that foils their art', when the minister arrived at the wake.

Orr was not only bilingual in lowland Scots and English, but he was obviously literate in both languages as well. His first spoken tongue was the 'braid Scotch' which he used until death, but in his writings (both for letters and poems), English was his usual medium. Hewitt maintained that when Orr wrote poetry, he seemed unable to go wrong when 'handling his native idiom'. Whether he should write in Scots or English was something of a quandry for Orr himself:

> *"My rude Scotch rhymes the tasteful justly slight,*
> *The Scotch-tongued rustics scorn each nobler fight'.*

In Orr's time there were few literary conventions for Scots, or even standard spellings for Scots words. Nevertheless, he seems to have been sufficiently aware of these to fall within the mainstream of contemporary Scots writing. Certainly this was also true in terms of the stanza forms he used. However even the modern Ulster-Scots native speaker will have considerable difficulty with Orr's rich Scots vocabulary. It probably will only be possible for most people today to understand Orr's Scots poems with the aid of a Scots dictionary (such as the *Concise Scots Dictionary*). In 1838, almost a generation after James Orr had lived in Ballycarry, the language of the Broadisland people was described vividly by the Ordnance Surveyors:

> *'Their accent, idioms and phraseology are strictly*
> *and disagreeably Scottish, partaking only of the*
> *broad and course accent and dialect of the Southern*
> *counties of Scotland'.*

Each of the two published books of Poems by James Orr

contains a section of songs at the end of the volume. Some of these individual works were simply titled 'Song', but the fact that they were indeed intended to be sung rather than recited, is confirmed by the titles of 'tunes' suggested for each piece. Assuming these tunes to have been well-known in Orr's day, they help us to understand the range of popular music then common in east Antrim. 'Green grow the Rushes, O', 'Come under my Plaidy', 'When bidden to the Wake or Fair', 'Roslin Castle', 'Humours of Glen', 'Burns Farewell', 'Savourna Deilish', 'Banks of Banna', 'Mary's Dream', 'Lochaber', 'Langolee', 'Plato's Advice', 'Free and Accepted Mason', and 'Vive la'. Clearly Scottish tunes dominated a sprinkling of English and Irish airs, but this is hardly surprising.

Orr evidently had a high regard for a of host of 'brother bards'. He was a close relative of Thomas Beggs of Ballynure, and a close friend of Samuel Thomson of Carngranny. He composed a Scots poem 'Epistle to S Thomson of Carngranny, A Brother Poet', in which he confirms that he sometimes visited 'Crambo Cave' where Thomson lived. Two other poems of Orr's were dedicated to poets, including an almost obligatory - but sincere - 'Elegy on the death of Mr Robert Burns, the Ayrshire Poet', and an 'Elegy on the death of Hugh Tynan, the Poet of Donaghadee'. Orr's name appears in the subscribers' lists for both of Thomson's 1793 and 1806 volumes of poems, and on Tynan's book of Posthumous Poems in 1803. Later, when Andrew M'Kenzie of Dunover in the Ards peninsula published a book of poems in 1811, Orr's name again appears in the subscribers' list. By the time Orr's monument was erected in 1831, the inscription only referred to the encouragement of 'the General Muse of his Brethren M'Kenzie, Beggs and English'. Needless to say, these were not the only 'brother-bards' of Orr, even in the fraternal sense of Freemasonry.

The subscribers' lists for Orr's own 1804 volume of poems is reproduced in full below. It is an intriguing list of the sorts of people prepared to order advance copies, and where those people lived. Almost 400 subscribers had agreed to pay for 570 copies of the book, and the most striking characteristic is the number of ordinary folk that were involved. Apart from half-a-dozen Presbyterian clergymen, the only other personages of note were two local landlords - Richard G Ker, Esq of Red Hall (Orr's own landlord), and Noah Dalway, Esq of Bella hill. The Dalways of Bellahill (or Dalway's Bawn) had a large estate on the Carrickfergus side of Ballycarry, and the only poem published by Orr that was addressed to any landlord was his 'Address to Noal Dalway, Esq' in his *Posthumous Works.* Orr never sought patronage from the landed gentry, and his poem to Dalway explains that 'A self-taught bard ... on a neighb'ring plain, High-minded DALWAY, thanks you for the praise (ill-earned, alas!) you gave his woodland lays'. Orr in his poem to Samuel Thomson gently rebukes him for seeking the patronage of the rich. The nearest Orr himself got to sycophancy was in the title of his poem 'The Glen, Descriptive of a delightful and romantic scene, in the estate of R Gervas Ker, Esq'. The bulk of Orr's subscribers - his real patrons - were the ordinary, local folk of east Antrim, and indeed this was the audience his poems were written for.

The poems themselves are a treasury of local information - much more than even the wealth of religious, political and dialect colour they provide for general Ulster history at the turn of the 18th century. However in selecting from Orr's works for this present volume, I trust that the omitted poems will not be regarded as being in any way inferior to those included.

PHILIP ROBINSON

SUBSCRIBERS' NAMES
(1804)

A

Rev. N. Alexander, Crumlin
J. Aiken, Islandmagee
Robert Aiken, do.
Mrs Allen, do.
George Allen, Loughmourne
John Allen, Ballycarry
A. Ardis, do.
Brice Allen, Broadisland
J. Askin, near Carrickfergus
Robert Agir, do.
John Alexander, do.
Dr. Aiken, do.
Mrs Anderson, do.
Edward Jones Agnew, Esq
    Kilwaughter
Charles Adamson, Stonyfall
James Addison, Knockagh
Thomas Addison, do.
Wm. Alexander, Ballynure
Andrew Alexander, do.
John Alexander, Doagh
Robert Allen, Dobbs-land
Miss A——, Belfast
Lawson, Annesley, do.

B

Rev. J. Bankhead, Broadisland,
    3 copies
A. Brennan, do.
A. Claney, do.
Miss Bankhead, do.
Miss Mary Bankhead, do
Miss Primrose Bankhead, do.

Miss Margaret Bankhead, do.
Thos. Brynan, Islandmagee
J. Brennan, do.
Joseph Barron, Loughmorne
R Barron, do.
S. Blair, near Glenoe
Miss M. Boyd, Broughshane
John Braidford, Carrickferg.
Mrs. Ann Boyd, do.
Mrs. Boya, do.
A. Brennan, do.
Wm. Bell, White-house
John Black, do.
John Blizzard, do.
Samuel Barron, Knockagh
Robert Barry, do.
A. Boyd, near Ballynure
E. Boyle, Larne
Sam. Brown, do.
James Blackwood, Belfast, 2 copies
John Bell, White-house
John Biggs, Ballycarry
Samuel Barron, do.
Thomas Boyle, Islandmagee
George Burleigh, Esq.
    Burleigh-hill
Mrs. Burleigh, do.
Miss Burleigh, do.
Edward Brice, Esq. Kilroot.

C

Thos. Campbell, Islandmagee
Miss Colvin, do.
John Corry, do.
N. Cameron, do.

Miss Jane Clark
Mrs. Crawford, Balloo
David Corrins, Glenoe
George Casement, Braid
Robert Crawford, do.
Wm. Close, Lisburn
Edm. Culbert, Broadisland
J. Close, Ballycarry
Miss Chisolm, near Carrickf.
Barn. Clark, do.
Miss A Crooks, Carrickfer.
Hugh Cunningham, do.
Miss E. Carley, do.
Rich. Chaplin, do.
Miss Craige, do.
Wm. Cary, do.
Miss Coburn, do.
Adam Cunningham, do.
John Close, do.
John Calwell, Maghramorne
William Carlisle, Raloo
Samuel Crow, near Ballynure
James Cudy, Belfast.

D

Mrs. Dickson, Belfast
Arthur Davis, Islandmagee
R. Downy, do.
William Drummond, Balloo
    4 copies
John Drummond, Drumbo
Thomas Dunn, Bellahill
Noah Dalway, Esq. do.
Mrs. Dalway, do.
Mrs. Davey, Sillytober
Sam. Davey, near Carrickfer.
Edward Davey, do.
James Davey, do.
Mrs, Davey, do.

John Dorman, do.
A. Donaldson, do.
John Dunlap, do.
Washington Dawson, do.
Wm. Davey, do.
Sam. Davey, do.
J. Dorman, Ballylaggen
Robert Dunlap, Belfast
James Drummond, do.

E

Henry Eccleston, Carrickfer.
John Frazer, do.
Mrs. Fitzsimons, do.
Henry Ellis, Esq. Prospect
Mrs. Ellis, do.

F

Sam. Falconbridge, Lisburn
Robert Fulton, do.
Robt. Finney, near Carrickf.
Wm. Finley, Esq. do.
Wm. Finley, Knockagh
Thomas Fry, White-house
Samuel Fulton, Carnmoney
John Fulton, do.

G

Wm. Gregg, Islandmagee
Geo. Grey, Glenoe
Wm. Gilbert, Loughmorne
J. Geddis, Ballytresna
Francis Gilmore, Ballyeaston
Thomas Gormal, Ballycarry
Miss Gordon, Larne
Hu. Gamble, Straid, 6 copies
Gwiley Carrickfergus

Victor Grant, Broadisland
Anna C Greaves, Carrickf.
Dean Greaves, do.
Arthur Gorman, do.
Jas. Gordon, do.
John Gormal, near Carrickf.
N. Gregg, Belfast
Thomas Grimshaw, Whitehouse
Joseph Grimshaw, do.
John Green, do.
Wm. Green, do.
Alex. Graham, do.
John Gray, do.

H

A. Hudson, Portglenone
Arthur Howard, Broadisland
Wm. Howard, do.
John Hay, Larne
John Heverin, Bellahill
James Hogshead, do.
John Hessan, do.
S. Hawthorn, Islandmagee
Thomas Hill, do.
Thos. Hill, do.
Thomas Houston, do.
John Hancock, Lisburn
John Herdman, do.
John Hay, Ballycarry
Miss Horsebro', do.
Mrs Houston, do.
Wm. Herdman, do.
Wm. Hamilton, near John
John Holmes, do.
Thos. Haggen, do.
Wm. Hamilton, do.
Dan. M. Haggen, do.
James Hunter, Belfast
G. Henesy, do.

Robert Hanley, do.
Wm. Harper, Carnmoney
R. Hamilton, near Carrick.
William Hanna, Ballycarry
Samuel Woodburn
Mrs. Hill, Knockagh
Rev. Adam Hill, Ballynure
James Hunter, Belfast
Mrs. Halliday, Belfast

I

Humphry Jameson, Belfast
Miss Jackson, Islandmagee
David Isdle, Lisburn
Mat. Jameson, near Carrickf.
James Irvine, Carrickfergus
Mrs Irvine, do.
George Johnston, Knockagh
Samuel Irvin, do.
Robt. Jelly, Lisbarnet
Miss Jones, Kilwaughter.

K

John Kean, Islandmagee
James Kelly, Glenoe
John Kennedy, Lisburn
John Kirk, near Carrickfer.
Mrs. A. Kirk, do.
Joseph Kirk, Knockagh
John Kirk, do.
Miss E. Kirk, Carrickfergus
Hugh Kirk, Belfast, 50 copies
Robt. Kirkwood, White-house
Rich. G. Ker, Esq. Red-hall
2 copies
R. Kennedy, Ballymaglaug.

L

James Laird, Islandmagee
James Long, do.
Chas. Livistone, Loughmorne
J. Lenard, Dublin
James Locke, Glenoe
Wm. Lettimore, Ballycarry
John Logan, Broadisland
Mrs. Logan, near Carrickf.
John Lettimore, do.
Wm. Lettimore, do.
John Lee, Carrickfergus
Isaac Lee, do.
John Lavery, do.
John Logan
John Lough, Larne, 2 copies.

M

John Mitchell, Kilroot
T. Molyneaux, Killead
Wm. Moore, jun. Larne, 2 copies
M. Morne, Book-club, 10 copies
Rev. J. Murphy, Islandmag.
I. Milliken, do.
John Martin, Balloo
Samuel Musgrave, Lisburn
Wm. Major, do.
N. Millar, Broadisland
A. Morrison, do.
J. Moore, do.
Richard Marron, Carrickfer.
John Moore, do.
Ezekiel Milliken, do.
Wm. Morrison, do.
Thomas Milliken, do.
Robt. Morrison, do.
Robt. Moore, do.
Mrs. Martin, do.
N Martin, Knockagh

John Mulholland, do.
J. Milliken, Ballyboley
A. Millar, near Ballynure
Robt. Mayne, White-house
Mrs. Munbee, North Lodge
Miss Major Brickfield
Edward Morris, Esq. Belfast

Mc

Miss M'Gowan, near Carrickfergus
William M'Ferron, do.
Rev. Geo. M'Claughey, do.
Robert M'Dowell, do.
John M'Keen, do.
Miss M'Gowan, do.
Hugh M'Dowell, do.
John M'Gill, Knockagh
Wm. M'Tamony, Carrickf.
D. M'Gowan, do.
Wm. M'Ferran, do.
J. M'Gowan, do.
J. M'Cullough, do.
Mrs. M'Cay, do.
Thomas M'Master, do.
J. M'Gill, Knockagh
Thos. M'Wherter, near Ballynure
Bryan, M'Cleverty, do. 6 copies
Adam M'Kittrick, Lisburn
Pat. M'Gowan, do.
Robert M'Cracken, do.
John M'Clure, do
J. M'Cauley, Crumlin
R. M'Cauley, do.
I. M'Kibben, Portaferry
Wm. M'Giffen, Broadisland
John M'Giffen, do.
Samuel M'Giffen, do.
Thomas M'Kee, do.
J. M'Dowell, do.
A. M'Kinstry, do.

A. M'Cammon, Islandmagee
James M'Ilwain, do.
Thomas M'Ilwain, do.
Miss M'Glaughlin, do.
Wm. M'Cullough, Balloo
J. M'Gowan, Martialtown
P. M'Avery, near Glenoe
Wm. M'Cullough, Braid
Miss M'Allister, do.
Robt. M'Bride, Ballycarry
Hugh M'Ferran, do
Edm. M'Clelland, do.
J. M'Kinley, do
Hercules M'Comb, Belfast
A. M'Donnell, M. D. do.
G. M'Pherson, do.
A. M'Clinton, White-house
John M'Gill, near Ballynure
John M'Cluney, Larne

N

Jackson Nelson, Islandmag.
Andrew Nelson, do.
Sam Nelson, Carrickfergus.

O

A. Orr, Broadisla.
John, Orr, do.
John Orr
John Orr
Matthew Orr
James Orr
William Orr, Ballybeen
Gawin Orr, Lisleen
James Orr, Muntogh
Ann Mary Orr
James Orr

P

Miss Pollock, Cross-hill
Miss Purdy, Martialtown
Thos. Penny, near Carrickf.
J. Parkhill, do.
Wm. Penny, do.
D. Penny, do.
Jas. Pinkerton, Broadisland
Wm. Penny, do.
John Parker, Broadisland
John Penny, Liverpool
Robert Patterson, Esq. Kilroot
John Pinkerton, Belfast
J. Poag, Bellahill

Q

James Quinn, Carrickfergus

R

Young Reany, White-house
J. Rea, Islandmagee
John Reid, do.
John Ross, near Carrickfer.
Wm. Ritchie, do
Miss Eliza Rogers, Carncoagh
James Rea, Maghramorne
Robert Rea, do.
James Reid
Robert Reid
Thos. Richards.

S

John Sims, White-house
S. Sanderson, near Carrickf.
Hugh Smyth, do.

Peter Savage, Carrickfergus
Dr. Stewart, do.
Edward Smyth, Esq. Larne
Wm. Simpson, do
James Smith, do.
Robert Stevenson, do.
Miss Sterling, do.
Wm. Service, do.
Miss Silliman, Islandmagee
James Spence, Lisburn
Wm. Steele, Ballycarry
James Steele, do.
Miss Steele, do.
George Stevenson, do.
A. Silliman, do.
J. Sanderson, do.
A. Service, Broadisland
Sam. Stewart, Loughmorne
James Scott, Ballynure,
          6 copies
Charles Stewart,
          near Carrickfergus
Smyth and Lyons', printers,
          Belfast, 50 copies
Wm. Skelton, do. 2 copies.

T

Sam. Thompson, Carngranny
Hugh Temple, Islandmagee
John Tole, Bellahill
Thos. Thompson, Carrickf.
John Thomson, do.
Andrew Thomson,
Claugnaduff
H. Thompson, Dublin
Robt. Trail, Belfast,
          50 copies

W

Robert White, Larne
A. Wilson, Broadisland
Miss Wheelan, do.
J. Wheelin, Crumlin
S. Whittle, Thistleboro'
Rev. J. Watson, Grey-abbey
Jas. Wilson, Islandmagee
John Wilson, do.
James Ward, Lisburn
J. Wilson, near Carrickfer.
Samuel Wiseman, do.
Miss Wallace, do.
Ezekiel Davis Wilson, Esq.
          Carrickfergus
Wm. Wilson, do.
Miss Wilson, do.
Thos. Whiteford, Ballylaggen
John White, Belfast.

–

Miss Margaret Christy, Kircassock
Miss Sarah Christy, do.
Mrs. Ann Christy, do.
Mr. James Christy, do.
Miss Isabella Shaw, Dundalk
Mr. James Thompson, Mahon,
          6 copies

TO THE POTATOE

I LEDGE we'd fen gif fairly quat o'
The weed we smoke, an' chow the fat o';
An' wadna grudge to want the wat o'
     Wealth-wastin' Tea;
But leeze me on the precious Pratoe,
    My country's stay!

Bright blooms the Bean that scents the valley,
An' bright the Pea, that speels the salie,
An' bright the Plumb tree, blossom't brawly,
     An' blue-bow't lint;
But what wi' straught rais't raws can tally,
    That sun-beams tint.

Waeworth the proud prelatic pack,
Wha Point an' Prataoes downa tak!
With them galore, an' whyles a plack
    To mak' me frisky,
I'll fen, an' barley freely lack -
    Except in whisky.

What wad poor deels on bogs an' braes,
Whase dear cot-tacks nae meal can raise;
Wha ne'er tase butter, beef or cheese,
     Nor pit new clais on;
While a' they mak' can har'ly please
    Some rack-rent messon.

What wad they do without *Do-black*s*,
Their weans wi' sarkless wames to rax?
They boost to forage like the fox
    That nightly plun'ers,
Or wi' the 'Squires turn out an' box,
    In hungry hun'ers.

A kind of the Potatoe

Sweet in the mornin', after dashlin',
Thy daigh is, pouther't owre wi' mashlin;
Creesh't scons stan' pil't on plates, or brislin'
    A' roun' the ingle,
While a fand *Wifie* fast is fislin,
     An tea-cups jingle.

Sweet to the boons that blythely enter
At dinner-time, the graise in centre,
Champ't up wi' kail, that pey the planter,
    Beans, pa'snips, peas!
Gosh! cud a cautious Covenanter
    Wait for the grace?

Sweet to the badger, aft a lander
At day-light-gaun, thou'rt on the brander,
Brown skin't, an' birslet. Nane are fander
    To hear thee crisp,
Ere in some neuk, wi' goose and gander
    He share the wisp

The weel-pair't peasants, kempin', set ye;
The weak wee boys, sho'el, weed, an' pat ye;
The auld guid men thy apples get ay
    Seedlin's to raise;
An' on sow'n-seeves the lasses grate ye,
    To starch their claes.

Then, in hin-hairst, when wee an' big ane,
Tak' to the fiel's, an' fa' a diggin',
Spades risp - tubs rumble - cars are jiggin' -
    L——d! what a noise is?
While monie a *pit's* prodigious riggin'
    High-archin', rises.

Thou feeds our beasts o' ilka kin',
The gen'rous steed, and grov'lin' swine:
An' poultry tribes; the doves ay fine,
    An' ducks besmear'd ay:
Dear was the man, an' half divine,
    Wha here first rear'd ye.

[2]

How comfortable, an' how couthy
We'd lieve, gif they wha bake cud brew thee!
Losh! 'twad be fine gif ilka youth ay,
                O' social tempers
Migh steep, an' still, for comrades drouthy
                A bing o' *hampers.* *

O Airlan! thou may weel be crouse,
Thy soger on his butter'd stews;
An' tar-breeks on the lab-scouse
                His ladle laves,
Can bear the gree frae hosts, an' crews,
                O' fine-fed knaves.

Upsettin' *England* sudna ding
Thee just sae sair - she's no the thing:
Gif thou'd withdraw for ae camping,
                Thy brow-beat callens,
Whaever pleas'd cud clip her wing,
                An' pare her talons.

What pity, folk thou sairst, sud tythe ay,
The poor mans rig, that maks him blythe aye!
May proud oppression ne'er come nigh thee,
                Nor sloth's fause smiles,
'Til time, wi' warl-destroyin' scythie
                Pass owre the isles!

* *Another kind of the Potatoe*

TEA

Celestial Tea! . . . a fountain that can cure
The ills of passion, and can free the fair
From sighs and frowns, by disappointment earn'd.
                    FERGUSON.

WELCOME, my frien's, - ye're just in time,
The kettle's on, an' soon will chyme;
An' gif, tho' us'd to strains sublime,
                    Ye'll listen me,
I'll clear my throat, an' rudely rhyme
                    In praise o' Tea.

What mak's ye nice? I'm no yet stintet
To mashlin beead an' weel-won mint to't;
The far-fetch'd leaf is maistly grantet
                    Sev'n times a week;
An' tak' my word, the day I want it
                    The pipe does reek.

Leeze me on Tea! - the maskin pot
Keeps peace about the poor man's cot:
Nae waitin' wife misca's the sot,
                    Wha stauchers hame wi'
A grain o' pouther an' o' shot,
                    To charge the wame wi' !

The L—d leuk on her wretched bield,
Whase pence are out, and hank unreel'd!
Nae griddle's het, nae pratoe peel'd,
                    To mak' a bap o't;
Nor *weed* nor *head-ach* tak's the field
                    Without a drap o't.

[4]

But blast the smuggler, fause an' fell,
Wha brews't in tinfu's by hersel;
An' bribes the sma'-craft no to tell
                    Their drudgin' daddy;
Deel nor he'd ay bounce in, pell-mell,
                    Just when 'tis ready.

When Riggie's yell, an' kitchen dear,
'Tis the poor cotter's cheapest cheer:
The creamless blash, that sugar fair
                    Has little share in,
Sen's glibly owre, his bonnoch bare,
                    An', saut, saut herrin.

The poorest bodies far or near,
Their pipes wi't ay on Sunday clear:
And a' the state-days o' the year;
                    But, chiefly, yule,
Wife, wean, an' cat, can hardly bear
                    To let it cool.

At breakin' clovin', kirn, an' quiltin',
'Tis ay the base that bliss is built on;
An' when the spae-wife to the Mill-town
                    In hiddlin's slips,
Without it, vain were her consultin'
                    Divinin' cups.

While roun' the hag the young things catch
The story o' their future match,
Tho' a' her skill's no worth a fitch,
                    Sud at her haunch
Bauld Moses rise to "slay the witch",
                    They'd mak' him gaunch.

When claughlin wives, wi' heads in flannin',
Forgether'd on a sabbath e'enin',
Pit spoonfu's twa a piece o' green in;
           (While wi' the mother
The splain an' stuffin' - a' compleenin'
                Sit whazzlin' throuther.)

Losh! how they rauner, rail, an' ripple
Their nybers names, an' mumph an sipple!
But, conscience! gif the auld delft nipple
           Nae ooze wad bring,
The priest, an' parish, king, an' people,
              Might tak their swing.

One wha oure-night has play'd the weary,
An' crept frae slumber, half deleery,
Wi' achin' banes, an' blinkers bleerie,
           An' tortur'd nerves:
While some slee jilt, wi' mirth sincere ay,
              His plight observes.

When wash'd his face, and camb'd his hair,
An' in again frae takin' air,
Sax reekin' rouns, or may be mair,
           Can mak' him able,
To think, an' speak, an' labour share,
              In barn or stable.

Yet "*Tea* mak's man a nerveless wrig,"
The doctor says — p-x on the prig!
Its juice has gladden'd monie a big,
           An' brave leel heart,
Wha'd firm as Gabbin keep the trig,
              Or forward dart -

But, harkee! there's a blyther singer;
I tald ye 'twad be nae lang hinger:-
Yestreen I daftly still'd the clangour
                 I' the auld twin'd blether;
Or Pints a piece o' something stronger
                 We'd bouse thegither.

ADDRESS TO BEER

O THOU! as sober an' serene,
As misty lake, or harvest e'en
Wha proves poor Airlan's frothless frien',
            In evil days;
The Bardie whom thou fill'd yestreen,
              Attempts thy praise.

But what's his praise! the warl agreed,
Has statues to less worth decreed:
Renown'd Reformer! thou hast freed
            Frae suff'rins tragic,
Unnumber'd fools, wha turn'd their head
            Wi' Whisky's magic.

He craz'd the banes o' sots ance stout,
An' wore to rags their hindmost suit;
He gied th' affront, when frien's fell out,
            Tho' kin' an' civil;
An' och! the parts o' bright repute
            He soon made drivil

He forc'd the Transport to depart;
An' dragg'd the Convict to the cart:
Nae 'missioned knave, wha in a mart
            Beat up fu' brisk ay,
Trepann'd the crowd wi' half the art
            O' captain Whisky.

E'en rocks wha scorn'd him, when a dint
He gied them, wad hae grogg'd a mint;
Gif Prudence, wi' a halsome hint,
            For ance procur'd thee,
Thy quart boost ay hae half a pint,
            Ere they endur'd thee.

But thae daft days are chang'd, in faith -
The punch glass dwarf, an' naggin baith,
As if on penance for the skaith
                  They brought on hashes,
Stan' idle, in the mournin' graith
                    O' dust an' ashes.

An' night an' day thy kettle's reekin',
For frien's wha call, thy favour seekin';
An' spen'thrifts, wont to stay a week in
                  The house o' pleasure,
On tenpence worth set hameward streekin,
                    An' hain their treasure.

Curs'd Blasphemy thou ne'er unfetters,
Nor sets base Slender on his betters;
Nae sot, owre thee, his geordies scatters
                  On rash daft bargains;
Nor fires his blood about State matters,
                  New psalms, an' organs.

Nane brawl rude sangs - nane rave - nane sleep -
Nor saw the sairs niest day they'll reap:
The mornin' dram, till times grow cheap,
                  E'en tiplers scorn;
An' in thy name their Shamrock steep
                  On Patrick's morn. -

The Muse thy pow'r inspires, is able
To spae thy triumphs will be stable;
For monie a pug wha scorn'd thy table,
                  Is turn'd a friend till't:
An' Folly e'en, when fashionable,
                  Mak's Wisdom bind tilt.

Tho' punch be trump 'mang nice tea-parties,
Whare Ceremony gloss'd wi' Art is,
I see the time - an' glad my heart is -
              When thy big jug,
Shall mak' them drap their bits o' carties,
              An' fill their mug.

An' now - whether folk choose to pull thee
Aff in cauld draughts, or warm, an' mull thee -
Whether wi' sugar'd sweets they duly
              Mix up an' skink thee,-
Or wi' strong pepper, hot as July,
              Ferment an' drink thee -

Ne'er may impolitic Taxation
Bring down thy envied estimation,
An' may nae frien' o' ERIN's nation -
              (She has ane here)
E'er want the price o' a potation
              O' guid cheap BEER!

TO A SPARROW

ON SEEING SOME BOYS ROB HER NEST

WEE, wanton, little thought o' birdie!
Pert, keen an' crouse, an unco wordie,
The stapple that sae lang has co'erd ye
      Your faes are seisin';
Shame fa' them! can they no afford ye
       The cauld house easin'?

What head o' wit, wi' sev'n years lear,
Cou'd mak' a nest sae feat, an' fair?
Eydent thou gather't grass an' hair,
       Frae daun till dark;
Fou scar'd, when school-boys chanc'd to stare
       Upo' thy wark.

Mony a day's hunger didst thou see,
While sittin' close as close cou'd be;
Yet now before thy anxious e'e
       They've rack'd thy housie,
An' made thy helpless familie
       The prey o' pousie.

E'enow thy breast is just as sair
As wife's wad be, wha'd see, or hear,
Sic fate, perforce, befa' her dear
       An' dauted weans;
But och! thy troublers dinna care
       How vast thy pains!

An' yet they're friety - sots wha'd gie
Their breasts, the swallows shield to be,
Deem't nae offence to harrie thee;
       Tho' minds mair noble
Wi' less remorse wad steal a tree,
       Than breed thee trouble.

Sae, when a wretched widow's sent
Frae some bit bield, whase leash is spent,
Tho' a' they hae be put to cant,
      She views it calmly,
Till rich, rude ruffians teaze and taunt
      Her gentle fam'ly.

Sae, when a carle, wi' mickle pains,
Scrapes up some gear to lea' his weans,
A band breaks in, an' bins the banes
      That late lay achin',
An' lea's him reft o' a' his gains,
      Sair-skaith'd, an' quakin'.

Sae, now there's monie suffrin' sair
By biggin' castles in the air,
But we twa will hae haudins there
      Sae lang's we've breath;
An' laugh at a' the sons o' care
      Wha sneak beneath.

Thou needna think this outrage odd,
For man's to man, like goose and tod;
But still the brave will rapine, blood,
      An' guile bewaur o',
An' spare the creature o' their God,
      Tho' but a Sparrow.

THE WANDERER

Tune - " Mary's Dream. "

"WHA's there?" she ax't. The wan'rers rap
      Against the pane the lassie scaur'd:
The blast that bray'd on *Slimiss* tap
      Wad hardly let a haet be heard.
"A frien'," he cried, "for common crimes
      "Tost thro' the country fore and aft" -
"Mair lown," quo' she - thir's woefu' times! -
      "The herd's aboon me on the laft."

"I call'd," he whisper'd, "wi' a wight
      "Wham aft I've help'd wi' han' an' purse;
"He wadna let me stay a' night -
      "Weel! sic a heart's a greater curse:
"But Leezie's gentler. Hark that hail!
      "This piercin' night is rougher far" -
"Come roun'," she said, "an' shun the gale,
      "I'm gaun to slip aside the bar."

Waes me! how wat ye're? Gie's your hat,
      An' dry your face wi' something - hae.
In sic a takin', weel I wat;
      I wad preserve my greatest fae:
We'll mak' nae fire; the *picquet* bauld
      Might see the light, an' may be stap;
But I'll sit up: my bed's no cauld,
      Gae till't awee an' tak' a nap.

WRITTEN IN WINTER

Tune - "Humours of Glen"

The green warl's awa, but the white ane can charm them
    Wha skait on the burn, or wi' settin' dogs rin:
The hind's dinlin' han's, numb't we snaw-baws, to warm them,
    He claps on his hard sides, whase doublets are thin.

How dark the hail show'r mak's yon vale, aince sae pleasin,!
    How laigh stoops the bush that's owre-burden't wi' drift!
The icicles dreep at the half-thow't house-easin',
    When blunt the sun beams frae the verge o' the lift.

The hedge-hauntin' blackbird, on ae fit whyles restin',
    Wad fain heat the tither in storm-rufflet wing;
The silly sweel't sheep, ay the stifflin' storm breastin',
    Are glad o' green piles at the side o' the spring.

What coof fir'd that shot? were you no far to blame, man,
    To pierce the poor Hare that was starvin' before:
Gif she wham ye court were like ane I'll no name, man,
    Her fine han' wad spurn ye, distin't sae wi' gore.

This night wi' the lass that I hope will be kin' soon,
    Wi' Sylvia, wha charms me, a wee while I'll stap:
Her e'e is as clear as the ice the moon shines on,
    As gentle her smile as the snaw-flakes that drap.

Perhaps she's now plannin', to pit a restriction
    Upon my profusion on niest new-years night,
To help some poor fam'lie on beds o' affliction,
    Without food or fuel, attendants or light.

Perhaps, singin' noo the dirge I tak' pride in,
    She thinks on the last storm, wi' pity an' dread -
How the spait crush't the cots - how Tam brak his leg slidin'.
    An' herds in the muir fand the poor pedlar dead.

'Tis guidness mak's beauty. The face ne'er was lo'esome,
    That weepsna whare woe is, and smilesna wi' glee.-
If Sympathy's strange to the saft female bosom,
    Its want's no made up by a bright cheek, or e'e.

THE SPAE-WIFE

Tune - "Come under my Plaidy."

YE frien's o' deep knowledge, if wise ye wad be,
Creep into my cave an' a' secrets ye'll see;
If maiden, or mother, *uncertainty* bother,
Frae doubt an' frae darkness, their min's I can free:
Ilk lass, no tald lees on, wha deems, an' wi' reason,
The youth she oblig't frae her fond arms will flee,
An' wife, in a fear ay, that jilts meet her dearie,
May learn the hale truth by applyin' to me.

Gif Chanticlear's ta'en frae the roost whare he craw't;
Or horse, kye, or sheep, frae the pasture-fiel' ca't,
My head I'll bestow ye, if I dinna shew ye
The leuks in a glass, o' the loun that's in faut:
Or else if ye cleek up, an' toss my delft tea cup,
If danger, or death's near, the gruns plain will shaw't:
By cuttin' o' cartes folk, an' no' by *black arts*, folk,
O past, present, future, I'll read ye a claut.

A spunkie reply't, wha oureheard the dark dame -
"Guid wife! they wha trust ye defeat their ain aim;
"The henpecket taupie, wha'd wiss to be happy,
"Sud ax nane wha ken - what the wife does at hame:
"Ilk sport-lovin' weary, might dread to come near ye,
"Wha ken'st the dark neuk whare she try't the blythe game -
"The grand plan of Nature's conceal'd frae a' creatures;
"Nor cud their skill chang't gif they kent the hale scheme.

"Ye promise promotion, an' sin' frae the mead
"The shepherd to sea, whare some shark soon he'll feed;
"The young thing, sae bonie, weds some canker't clownie,
"Because ye've presag'd that nae ither's decreed -
"While dupes trust the *sybil* far mair than the bible,
"An' change the last sixpence that ye may be fee'd,
"I'll scorn *the to-morrow*, an' banishin' sorrow,
"Learn mair light frae *whiskey* than e'er fill't your head.

THE PASSENGERS

Down where yon anch'ring vessel spreads the sail
That idly waiting, flaps with ev'ry gale;
Downward they move, a melancholy band,
Pass from the shore, and darken all the strand.
                              GOLDSMITH.

How calm an' cozie is the wight,
    Frae cares an' conflicts clear ay,
Whase settled headpiece never made,
    His heels or han's be weary!
Perplex'd is he whase anxious schemes
    Pursue applause, or siller,
Success nor sates, nor failure tames;
    Bandied frae post to pillar
                Is he, ilk day.

As we were, Comrades, at the time
    We mov't frae Ballycarry,
To wan'er thro' the woody clime
    Burgoyne gied oure to harrie:
Wi' frien's consent we prie't a gill,
    An' monie a house did call at,
Shook han's an' smil't; tho' ilk fareweel
    Strak, like a weighty mallet,
                Our hearts, that day.

On shore, while ship-mates halt, tho' thrang't,
    Wi' lasses hearts to barter;
Nybers, an' frien's, in boatfu's pang't,
    Approach our larboard quarter;
Syne speel the side, an' down the hatch
    To rest, an' crack, an' gaze on
The boles o' births, that monie a wratch
    Maun squeeze in, for a season,
                By night, an' day.

"This is my locker, yon'ers Jock's,
    "In that auld creel, sea-store is,
"Thir births beside us are the *Lockes**,
    "My uncle's there before us;
"Here hang my tins an' vitriol jug,
    "Nae thief's at han' to meddle 'em" -
"L—d, man, I'm glad ye're a' sae snug;
    "But och! 'tis owre like Bedlam
                  Wi' a' this day.

"All boats ashore!" the mate cries stern,
    Wi' oaths wad fear a saunt ay:
"Now Gude be wi' ye, Brice, my bairn" -
    "An' Gude be wi' ye, Auntie."
What *keep-sakes*, an' what news are sent!
    What smacks, an' what embraces!
The hurryin' sailors sleely sklent
    Droll leuks at lang wry faces,
                  Fu' pale that day.

While "Yo heave O!" wi' monie a yell
    The birkies weigh the anchor;
Ilk mammies pet conceits itsel'
    The makin' o' a Banker;
They'll soon, tho', wiss to lieve at hame,
    An' dee no worth a totam,
When brustin' breast, an' whamlin' wame,
    Mak' some wise men o' Gotham
                Cry halt! this day.

*A family who sailed for America in 1798

Some frae the stern, wi' thoughts o' grief
    Leuk back, their hearts to Airlan';
Some mettle't bucks, to work ay brief,
    At en's o' rapes are harlin';
Some haud aback frae dangers brow
    Their toddlin' o'er, no cautious;
An' some, wi' monie a twine an' throe,
    Do something wad be nauceous
                To name, this day.

Meanwhile, below, some count their beads,
    While prudes, auld-light sit cantin';
Some mak' their beds; some haud their heads,
    An' cry wi' spite, a' pantin' !-
"Ye brought us here ye luckless cauf!
    ("Aye did he; whisht my darlin'!)
L—d sen' me hame! wi' poke an' staff,
    "I'd beg my bread thro' Airlan',
                My lane, that day."

In twathree days the maist cam' to,
    Few heads were sair or dizzy;
An' chiel's wha scarce a turn cud do,
    Begoud to be less lazy:
At night (to tell amang oursel's)
    They crap, wi' fandness fidgin',
To court - or maybe something else,
    Gif folk becam' obligin',
                Atween an' day.

Roun' the cambouse what motley ban's
    At breakfast-time cam' swarmin' !
Tin, tankards, kettles, pots, an' pans,
    The braid flat fire was warmin':
The guid auld rule, "first come first ser't,"
    Was urg't by men o' mettle;
An' ay whan callens grew mislear't,
    The arm o' flesh boost settle
                Th' affray, that day.

A bonie sight I vow it was,
    To see on some lown e'nin',
Th' immense, smooth, smilin' sea o' glass,
    Whare porpoises were stenin':
To see at night the surface fine
    That Cynthia made her path on;
An' snove, an' snore thro' waves o' brine,
    That sparkle't like a heath on
                A bleaze some day.

But now a gale besets our bark,
    frae gulph to gulph we're tumble't;
Kists, kits, an' fam'lies, i' the dark,
    Wi' ae sidejerk are jumble't:
Some stauchrin' thro' a pitch lays laigh -
    Some, drouket, ban the breaker;
While surge, on surge, sae skelps her - Hegh!
    Twa three like that will wreck her
                A while ere day.

Win's, wives, an' weans, rampage an' rave,
    Three score at ance are speakin';
While blacks wha a' before them drave,
    Lye cheepin' like a chicken -
"What gart us play? or bouse like beasts?
    "Or box in fairs wi' venom?"
Hear how the captain laughs an' jests,
    An' bit a bord between him
                An' death, this day.

'Tis calm again. While rightin' things,
    The heads o' births are bizziet,
The seaman chews his quid, an' sings,
    An' peys his frien's a visit -
"Eh! dem my eyes! how is't, goodman?
    "Got clear of *Davy's* locker?
"Lend me a facer till we lan',
    "Til blind as Newgate's knocker
                We'll swig, that day."

Here, gash guidmen, wi' nightcaps on,
    At ance baith pray an' watch;
An', there, for light, sits monie a loun
    At Cartes beneath the hatch;
Here, some sing sangs, or stories tell,
    To ithers bizzy knittin';
An', there some readin' to themsels,
    Nod owre asleep, while sittin'
                Twa fold that day.

Now Newfoun'lan's becalmin' banks
    Our ship supinely lies on;
An' monie a ane his lang line fanks,
    Whase heuk some captive dies on:
An' now, disguis't, a fore-mast-man
    Shaves dry, the churls unwillin'
To pay the poll-tax on deman'-
    A pint, or else a shillin'
              A piece, that day.*

Aince mair luck lea's us (plain 'tis now
    A murd'rer in some mess is)
An English frigate heaves in view,
    I'll bail her board, an' press us:
Taupies beneath their wives wha stole,
    Or 'mang auld sails lay flat ay,
Like whitrats peepin' frae their hole,
    Cried, "is she British, wat ye,
              Or French, this day?"

'Twas but a brig frae Baltimore,
    To Larne wi' lintseed steerin';
Twa days ago she left the shore,
    Let's watch for lan' appearin':
Spies frae the shrouds, like laigh dark clouds,
    Descried domes, mountains, bushes;
The Exiles griev't - the sharpers thiev't-
    While cronies bous't like fishes,
              Conven't, that day.

Whan glidin' up the *Delaware*,
    We cam' forenent *Newcastle*,
Gypes co'ert the wharf to gove, an' stare,
    While out, in boats, we bustle:
Creatures wha ne'er had seen a black,
    Fu' scar't took to their shankies;
Sae, wi' our best rags on our back,
    We mixt amang the Yankies,
                An' skail't, that day.

It has been a long established custom for the seamen, on reaching the banks of Newfoundland, to exact a shilling, or a shilling's worth of liquor, from every passenger; and to shave, without soap, those who refuse to contribute their quota.

THE BULL-BEAT

IF e'er the poet, pity's child,
Forsakes his spirit-soothing lyre,
And joins the sport with comrades wild,
He oft deplores while they admire;
While they torment, he now wou'd save
The landscape's monarch, bold and brave.

Confin'd amid th' assembling crowd,
Sedate and sad, the victim stands;
The mastiff eyes the man of blood,
And panting, waits his fell commands;
And lo! keen rushing from the slip,
The lordly brute they fiercely grip.

While one obliquely pulls his tongue,
Another tears his ample chest,
A third is at his shoulder hung,
And different posts employ the rest:
Just as we've seen the human herd
Mangle a brave man, singly fear'd.

Unmov'd, he now stands torture-proof,
Now madly on his foes he bounds;
His horn rips some, and some his hoof,
That, archly pawing, foils the hounds:
Heard you that groan? - how vast his pain! -
What noble strife has been in vain!

Firm, tho' forlorn, and bent to make
One glorious effort, ere he yield,
He darts intrepid from the stake,
And falls abruptly on the field:
Huzzas and howls, at once ascend;
Foam, gore and mud, together blend.

And now the butcher aims his piece,
And firing, ends the suff'rer's life -
Can men endure such scenes as these?
Can christians pride in gore and strife?
Such scenes amuse the slave and sot;
And saints and heroes shun the spot.

THE POOR-HOUSE

AN ELEGY

He feeds yon alms-house, neat, but void of state,
Where Age and Want, sit smiling at the gate.
POPE

WITH pensive steps I seek yon lofty dome,
       That on the height is seen to glow and gleam -
Rear'd by the bounteous, as a peaceful home,
       Where indigence and age, might shelter claim.

Hail, blest asylum! where at once we find
       A seminary, shop, and place of pray'r:
Sees Heav'n a worthier sight, than when the kind
       The well-timed boon to mis'ry's children share?

Well pleas'd these comfortable rooms I trace,
       Where age and childhood earn and eat their bread,
While competence consents once more to grace
       The congregated poor who lately stray'd.

Here, while Extravagance! thy sober'd slave
       Brands thy bright temples as he plies his task,
Misfortune's worthier victim, bow'd, yet brave,
       Earns the blest bread he ne'er would deign to ask.

There, while the orphan, far from kindred's care,
       Learns truth and science - learns to live and die,
The widow'd mother, on the wings of pray'r,
       Surmounts the earth, and communes with the sky.

Who would not pity? have we health and state?
       Are are not many here who had the same? -
Disease may seize us on the hour of fate
       That all our fortune sinks in flood or flame.

Who would despise them? many a child now here,
    May climb the height from which his father fell;
May woo the muses, charm the public ear,
    Or teach the tide of battle where to swell.

Blest Charity! while vagrant pests prepare
    Ropes for their necks, and for their souls the flame,
Thy sons serve earth and heaven. A little care
    Makes them their country's pride, who were her shame.

What ghastly groups, diseas'd, around me stand!
    Dull headach droops, spleen frets, consumption wastes,
And dotage wildly stares, while palsy's hand
    Flings o'er his head the meal he seldom tastes.

The beldame pants, that's gasping asthma's prey,
    The rheum-rack'd soldier pines, but ne'er complains;
The tar crawls by, whose limbs felt frosts stern sway -
    Hark how they talk of shipwrecks and campaigns!

No more the belle shall charm thy sons of mirth,
    No more the hearty tar shall heave the lead,
No more the drum shall call the soldier forth,
    To serve his country where the valiant bleed.

No more domestic peace, (by transient strife
    Made thrice more valu'd) shall their homes attend:
Adown th' abrupt declivity of life,
    They feebly totter to their journey's end.

My heart forebodes that I, ere life shall cease,
    A poor old man, the last of all my race,
Coughing along, and shouldering the breeze,
    May seek sad refuge in some kindred place.

There, far remov'd from ev'ry hope and fear;
    Recite the scenes of youth, so like a dream,
Till death conclude the winter of my year,
    And give the dust my weary, willing frame.

THE IRISH COTTIER'S DEATH AND BURIAL

> " — *Nurs'd in the peasant's lowly shed,*
> *To hardy independence bravely bred;*
> *By early poverty to hardship steel'd,*
> *And train'd to arms in stern misfortune's field .*"
> > *BURNS.*

ERIN! my country! preciously adorn'd
      With every beauty, and with every worth,
Thy grievances through time shall not be scorn'd,
      For powerful friends to plead thy cause step forth:
      But more unblest, oppression, want, and dearth,
Did during life, distressfully attend
      The poor neglected native of thy North,
Whose fall I sing. He found no powerful friend,
'Till Death was sent by Heaven to bid his soul ascend.

The blameless Cottier, wha his youth had pass'd
      In temperance, an' felt few pains when auld,
The prey o' pleurisy, lies low at last,
      And aft his thoughts are by delirium thrall'd:
      Yet while he raves, he prays in words weel wal'd,
An' mutters through his sleep o' truth an' right;
      An' after pondering deep, the weans are tald
The readiest way he thinks they justly might
Support themsels thro' life, when he shall sink in night.

Wi' patient watchfu'ness, lasses an' lads,
      Carefu' an' kin', surroun' his clean caff bed,
Ane to his lips the coolin' cordial ha'ds,
      An' ane behin' supports his achin' head;
      Some bin' the arm that lately has been bled,
An' some burn bricks his feet mair warm to mak;
      If e'er he doze, how noiselessly they tread!
An' stap the lights to mak the bield be black,
An' aft the bedside lea, an' aft slip saftly back.

Rang'd roun' the hearth, where he presides nae mair,
      Th' inquirin' nybers mourn their sufferin' frien';
An' now an' then divert awa their care,
      By tellin' tales to please some glaiket wean,
      Wha's e'e soon fills whan told about the pain
Its sire endures, an' what his loss wad be;
      An' much they say, but a', alas! in vain,
To soothe the mither, wha ha'f pleas'd could see
Her partner eas'd by death, though for his life she'd die.

And while they're provin' that his end is sure
      By strange ill omens - to assuage his smart
The minister comes in, wha' to the poor,
      Without a fee performs the doctor's part:
      An' while wi' hope he soothes the suff'rer's heart,
An' gies a cheap, safe recipe, they try
      To quat braid Scotch, a task that foils their art;
For while they join his converse, vain though shy,
They monie a lang learn'd word misca' an' misapply.

An' lo! the sick man's dyin' words to 'tend,
      Th' alarm'd auld circle gather roun', an' weep;
Deceiv'd by hope, they thought till now he'd mend,
      But he thought lang in death's embrace to sleep.
      "Let ithers will," he says, "a golden heap,
I can but lea my blessin' an' advice -
      Shield your poor mither, an' her counsel keep;
An' you, my senior sons, that ay were wise,
Do for my late born babes, an' train them for the skies.

"Be honest an' obligin'; if ye thrive
      Be meek; an' firm whan crosses come your road;
Should rude men wrang ye, to forgie them strive;
      An' gratefu' be for benefits bestow'd:
      Scorn nae poor man wha bears oppression's load,
Nor meanly cringe for favours frae the proud;
      In ae short sentence - serve baith man an' God.
Sae, whan your clay lies mould'rin' in a shroud,
Your saul shall soar to Heaven, an' care nae mair becloud."

His strength here fail'd, but still affection's e'e
    Spak on; a moment motionless he lay;
Bade "Peace be wi' them!" turn'd his head awee,
    And pass'd through death's dark vale without dismay.
    The speechless widow watch'd the stiff'ning clay,
And shed some "nat'ral tears" - rack'd, yet resign'd;
    To loud laments the orphan groupe gied way,
An' mourn'd, unfelt, the wants an' wrangs they'd find,
Flung friendless on the warl, that's seldom unco kind.

Come hither, sons of Plenty! an' relieve
    The bonny bairns, for labour yet owre wee,
An' that mild matron, left in life's late eve,
    Without a stay the ills o' age to dree:
    Had I your walth, I hame wad tak' wi' me
The lamb that's lookin' in my tear-wat face;
    An' that dejected dame should sit rent free
In some snug cot, that I wad hae the grace
To visit frequently, and bid her hardships cease.

Cou'd he whose limbs they decently hae stretch'd,
    The followers o' freets awake an' mark,
What wad he think o' them, he oft beseeched
    To be mair wise than mind sic notions dark?
    To bare the shelves o' plates they fa' to wark;
Before the looking-glass a claith they cast;
    An' if a clock were here, nae ear might hark
Her still'd han's tell how hours an' moments pass'd;
Ignorance bred sic pranks, an' custom gars them last.

But see what crowds to wauk the Cottier come!
    Maist frae respect, but some to gape-seed saw:
Douce men an' wives step forward to the room,
    The youths on forms sit rang'd roun' ilka wa';
    Some at a plate light pipes as white as snaw;
Some hark in neuks wi' lasses whom they prize;
    Some banter simple nymphs, their parts to shaw;
But though a laugh be sometimes like to rise,
They dinna either death or the deceas'd despise.

Belyve an auld man lifts the Word o' God,
    Gies out a line, an' sings o' grief an' pain;
Reads o'er a chapter, chosen as it should,
    That maks them sure the dead shall rise again;
    An' prays, that he, wha's hand has gie'n and ta'en,
May be the orphan's guide, the widow's stay;
    An' that, rememb'rin death ere health be gane,
They a' may walk in wisdom's Heaven-ward way,
Like him, the man o' worth, that's now a clod o' clay.

An' now a striplin', wi' becomin grace,
    Han's the wauk-supper, in a riddle, roun';
Hard bread, an' cheese, might nicest palates please,
    Bought frae a huxter in the nyb'rin' town;
    An' gi'es them gills a piece o' rum sae brown,
By polished sots wi' feign'd reluctance pried;
    Though here an' there may sit a menseless loun,
The thoughtfu' class consider poor folks need,
An' only "kiss the cup," an' hardly ance break bread.

While thus they sit, the widow lifts the sheet,
    To kiss the corps that worms will shortly gnaw;
Some argue Scripture - some play tricks - some greet;
    Here they're asleep - an' there they slip awa'.
    Folk wha lay list'ning 'till the cock wad craw,
Now rise frae rest, an' come to sit a while;
    Salute their frien's, and speer for their folk a',
An' to the fire step ben, frae which a file
O' warmer rustics rise, polite in simplest stile.

Syne wi' anither glass they hail day-light,
    An' crack mair cruse o' bargains, farms, an' beasts;
Or han' tradition down, an' ither fright,
    Wi' dreadfu' tales o' witches, elves, an' ghaists.
    The soger lad, wha on his pension rests,
Tells how he fought, an' proudly bares his scaur;
    While unfledg'd gulls, just looking owre their nests,
Brag how they lately did their rivals daur,
Before their first sweethearts, an' dashed them i' the glaur.

An' while some lass, though on their cracks intent,
    Turns to the light and sleely seems to read,
The village sires, wha kent him lang, lament
    The dear deceas'd, an' praise his life an' creed;
    For if they crav'd his help in time o' need,
Or gied him trust, they prov'd him true an' kin';
    "But he," they cry, "wha blames his word or deed,
Might say the sun, that now begins to shine,
Is rising i' the wast, whare he'll at e'en decline."

Warn'd to the Cottier's burial, rich an' poor
    Cam' at the hour, tho' win' an' rain beat sair;
An' monie met it at the distant moor,
    An' duly, time-about, bore up the bier,
    That four men shouther'd through the church-yard drear.
Twa youths knelt down, and humbly in the grave
    Laid their blest father. Numbers shed a tear,
Hop'd for an end like his, and saftly strave
To calm his female frien's, wha dolefully did rave.

An' while the sexton earth'd his poor remains,
    The circling crowd contemplatively stood,
An' mark'd the empty sculls, an' jointless banes,
    That, cast at random, lay like cloven wood:
    Some stept outbye, an' read the gravestanes rude,
That only tald the inmates' years an' names;
    An' ithers, kneeling, stream'd a saut, saut flood,
On the dear dust that held their kinsfolks' frames -
Then, through the gate they a' pass'd to their diff'rent hames.

ERIN! my country! while thy green sward gilds
    The good man's grave, whose fall I strove to sing,
Ten thousand Cottiers, toiling on thy wilds,
    Prize truth and right 'bove ev'ry earthly thing:
    Full many a just man makes thy work-shops ring;
Full many a bright man strips thy meads to mow;
    Closer in thy distress to thee they cling;
And though their fields scarce daily bread bestow,
Feel thrice more peace of mind than those who crush them low.

THE FOUNDERED FARMER
OR
THE FATE OF INTEMPERANCE

O! HAD not LAURENCE lov'd too well
    Enchanting pleasure, false as fair,
Long on the landscape where he fell,
    He might have flourish'd, free from care.

The night in snow had wrapt the earth,
    And lock'd the streams in icy chain;
When, reeling from the house of mirth,
    He stole from an inebriate train.

But never on another friend
    His kind eye glanc'd a placid ray;
Nor did his long-look'd entrance end
    His parent's care, who mourn'd his stay.

Ne'er did he softly lift the latch,
    As his fond fair the bar drew by:-
Expectant maid! in vain you watch,
    For his return, who soon shall die!

Ah! when they heard the north wind lift
    Its dreadful notes, how deep they groan'd!
And when they marked the stifling drift,
    Despair, too justly, Hope dethron'd.

Yet, had wrong'd reason been his guide,
    He might have kept the dang'rous way;
But through the moss he turned aside,
    And perish'd in a pit of clay.

When rain th' appaling place had bar'd,
    The hinds bore home his corse so white,
Before they cautiously prepared
    His kindred for the shocking sight.

His mother swoon'd upon his bier,
    And sick'ning, soon resign'd her life;
In silent grief - the most severe -
    The father mourn'd his son and wife.

The maid, whose thoughts his absence tir'd,
    (For she had nam'd their nuptial day,)
By chance was there, and phrenzy fir'd
    Her soul, that sense no more will sway.

And his companions, pain'd in heart,
    Praise his lost worth, and fondly show
That social friendship, loth to part,
    The folly caus'd that laid him low.

Ye slaves of wine! that guardian bless,
    Who from mischance yet keeps you free;
See, how one hour of wild excess
    May cause an age of misery!

How many of my countrymen,
    Like him whose fall these numbers tell,
In rude Intemp'rance' haunted den,
    Hear want, scorn, ruin, round them yell!

O my kind country! wise, as warm,
    Prudence with pleasure still connect;
And, firmly resolute, reform
    Your only national defect.

THE PERSECUTED NEGRO

The House of Assembly, in this Island, have passed a law which says -
"No Missionary, Sectary, or others, shall presume to teach our slaves,
under the penalty of £20 for every slave found in their Chapels, &c.
and three months imprisonment."
        See a Letter from Jamaica, in a late publication.

WISDOM's spurn'd, and lonely silence
      Keeps our Chapel clos'd by pride.
What was heard, that, Chiefs! your vi'lence
      Parts the Negro and his Guide?
Did you think to keep us pray'rless,
      Lest Heav'n's King should hear our cry?
Or that Truth would make us fearless
      In the cause of Liberty?

Impious men! had Fortune made you
      Slaves in Africa, many a Chief,
Charitably would persuade you
      To embrace his false belief;
You, who should be heard deploring
      Our wild errors, wield your rod,
To prevent us from adoring,
      With yourselves, the living GOD.

When to "teach all human creatures,"
      Truth's disciples orders got,
Was it added - "Mark the features
      "Of the slave, and 'mend him not."
GOD, whose pity sees the sparrow
      Perish, as 'tis earthward roll'd,
Values this poor soul you "harrow"
      More than all your island's gold.

Droves of slaves expos'd to auction,
    Ne'er made your hard hearts so vain,
As would ours be, were instruction
    Granted our misguided train:
If in them you'd knowledge cherish,
    We'd to Ignorance submit;
You'll be punish'd if they perish;
    To improve them we're unfit.

In the host that wooes commotion,
    In the sea-encircled fleet,
In the dungeon, pure devotion
    Gives the Good communion sweet:
Ev'ry wretch, in ev'ry region,
    May inquire for heav'nly truths,
Save the Negro; him Religion,
    With her Sabbath never soothes.

Mayn't the meanest in the nations
    That debasement deepest galls,
When they see all rank's gradations
    End at once, when Worship calls;
And 'tis deem'd no rude intrusion
    To approach the proud man's pew,
Pray to 'scape the persecution
    Our souls suffer for our hue?

Never may the Missionary,
    When sore toil at night we leave,
Promise Heav'n's rest to the weary,
    And Heav'n's freedom to the slave;
Ne'er, with anxious expectation,
    From the book we'll hear him read,
How poor tribes, forc'd from their nation,
    From Captivity were freed.

Thou! who scorn'd'st not with our features
  To create a deathless part;
Curbing our outrageous natures,
  May we shine, when white men smart!
And, though they prolong our blindness,
  Who should light for us provide;
Let thy peace-imparting kindness,
  Be our hearts' immediate guide!

THE READING SOCIETY

The sun has set in smiles, and pensive eve
    Sheds soft'ning dew-drops on the thirsty soil;
The slow-pac'd swains the cultur'd landscape leave,
    And from their work-shop stalk the sons of toil.

My sweet associates, kind in thought and looks,
    Who all my toils, and all my pastimes share;
Attend the reading circle with your books,
    And sensibly converse away your care.

We'll briefly criticise the page that taught
    Us worth or wit, and at the mental feast,
Transfusing copiously the stream of thought,
    Revive its spirit, and improve its taste.

Howe'er in taste or understanding form'd,
    We here are gratified in works of worth;
Whether with fiction or with truth we're charm'd,
    Divinity or morals, sense or mirth.

GIBBON and HUME to history's friend record
    The fall of ancient states, and rise of new;
Elab'rate JOHNSON gives the rustic bard
    The Poets' Lives, whose works he here may view.

The vet'ran, WASHINGTON to vict'ry took,
    May in his life renew each grand campaign;
The far-sail'd tar may lift thy Voyage, COOKE!
    And circumnavigate the world again. -

But, hark! the question giv'n, we now commence
    The kind debate, and he whose "lucky hit"
To silence awes some son of eloquence
    Is proud as FOX exulting over PITT.

How fond of order, he who fills the chair!
    How courteous and correct each humbler hind!
Not one will interrupt, insult, or swear -
    True to the rules that all at entrance sign'd.

Ye sons of pow'r! how can ye say we err
    By such pursuits, though us no gains they've brought:
Though toil supports us, why will ye infer,
    That knowledge, therefore, can avail us nought?

Who are the men, that, summon'd to th' assize,
    With cautious candour testify the truth?
They, who can noise and insolence despise,
    To speak in crowds inur'd in early youth.

Who are the men who tempting bribes oppose,
    When cringing candidates their suffrage court?
They who have nobly learn'd, from books like those,
    To prize the rights you promise to support.

Fam'd Greece! whose valour yet in story shines,
    And will through time, if worth can writing save,
Did not more feebly form th' intrepid lines,
    That taste and love adorn'd her soldiers brave.

Nor was Helvetia, in whose cantons rude,
    A wond'rous change by industry was wrought,
The easier by degen'rate Gaul subdu'd,
    That her wrong'd peasants wisely read and thought.

Then sons of pow'r! who've lately deign'd to make
    The culture of the field your favour find;
Go on, in Heav'n's blest name, and undertake
    A nobler task - the culture of your kind!

For us in humbler walks, we'll spend our time
    In honest toil, or with a book and friend,
Still farther up the hill of knowledge climb,
    And bless the hands that help us to ascend.

And should soul-trying strife command our sword,
    Or sorrow crave our succour, soon you'll find,
Whether the slaves of ignorance abhorr'd,
    Or men of sense, have hearts more brave and kind.

BALLYCARRY

"Loveliest village of the plain,
Where health and plenty cheer the lab' ring swain."
                                        GOLDSMITH.

My native village! many a lay
        Have scenes less lovely claim'd from me;
How could I ev'ry hour survey
        Thy sweets so priz'd, and silent be?
Happy thy tribes! while Fortune's tides
        Fast-ebbing, strand the sons of glory;
Our humbler life, unting'd by strife,
        Glides smoothly on in Ballycarry.

Sublimity stalks on the hill
        That shields thee from th' inclement gale;
And beauty smiles beside the rill,
        Which intersects thy fertile vale.
Thy swains embrace, and bless the place -
        If on some morn they strangely vary,
The world's bright eye is clos'd in joy,
        While friendship sports in Ballycarry.

At yon old ruin, 'midst a throng
        Whose lives, tho low, from truth ne'er swerv'd,
Lie men once great whose sword and tongue,
        In camp and senate, Erin serv'd:
There thy rever'd forefathers heard
        The first Dissenter dar'd to tarry
On Erin's plains, where men felt pain
        For conscience sake, in Ballycarry.

How sweet to see the sons of grace,
        Thy temple throng on Sabbath morn!
How sweet to see the infant race,
        That, cherub-like, thy school adorn!
Let not the great, who rule the state,
        Despise thee, their poor tributary;
The loom and wheel, both plied with zeal,
        Raise rent, tax, tithe, in Ballycarry.

Much thou'lt improve. - The poor man's child
    The Sunday-school shall blestly train
Thy reading-club, the rustics wild
    Shall join, and knowledge cheaply gain:
Thy tradesman's fun, ne'er proudly shunn'd,
    Shall serve the sick, with prudence wary;
And thy fair mart, shall yield desert,
    The premium earn'd in Ballycarry.

Yes, Hope now opes before my eyes
    A vista to futurity;
I see bright domes in thee arise,
    Where great, good men, shall live and die -
Yon towns sublime, that gild our clime,
    Were once, like thee, unnam'd in story;
But worth divine has made them shine,
    And shine she'll make thee, Ballycarry.

Eye that fine scene before you range,
    Wild wand'rer! eye that scene, and say,
Will e'er migration's spirit strange
    Entice thy steps from home to stray?
Stay! if pure peace thou would'st embrace,
    Peace here has not one adversary;
Should strife abhorr'd unsheath the sword,
    Stay! and contend for Ballycarry.

BALLYCARRY FAIR

Tune - "Green grow the Rashes, O."

SIN' sunrise drudgin' i' the moss,
    I've dearly bought a shillin', O;
An' ho' to me a weighty loss,
    To spen it I'm fu' willin' 0:
Sae I'se refit and want my rest,
    Tho' I'm baith wat an' weary, O;
For now the fair is at the best
    In sportsome Ballycarry, O.

CHORUS
Hartsome is the claughin, O,
Hartsome is the claughin, O,
Where ev'ry hour I hae to spare
Is past in mirth and laughin', O.

The ginge-bread wife, that's now as drunk's
    An owl; the herds new whistle, O;-
The bumpkin beau, wi' pouther't funks,
    Like Downs upon a thristle, O-
Then men o' strength wha bullets play,
    Or putt in ilka alley, O;
An' circles warpin' to and frae,
    Mak' a' the spirits rally, O.
                  Hartsome is, &c.

The winsome wean, wi' heart fu' light,
    Smiles up, an' seeks a fairin, O;
The armless beggar craves a mite
    Whare'er he gains a hearin', O,
What tho' they'll waste whate'er we gie
    On *sweeties*, an' a *drappie*, O!
We'se gie them something; ae babee
    Apiece, wad mak them happy, O.
                  Hartsome is, &c.

What clusters pauvice roun' the stalls
  Whare pedlars streek their conscience, O!
An' whare the ballad-singer bawls
  A string o' noisy nonsense, O!
But sunset's come, an' aged ban's
  Step hameward at their leisure, O;
While younger folk mak' Herdman's* han's
  Unlock the springs o' pleasure, O.
      Hartsome is, &c.

Now earth revolvin' turns up night,
  The lanely streets' forsaken, O,
An' wine, an love, an' frien'ship bright,
  Mak' hearts, aince cauldrife, waken, O:
Now bargains, courtships, toasts, huzzas,
  Combine in blythe disorder, O;
While *pairs* play pranks in Archy's wa's
  That I'll be nae recorder o'
      Hartsome is, &c.

The sot lays down his head to sleep,
  The crabbit sumph sits snarlin', O;
This treats a lass wham that will keep,
  An' slap! they're up an' quarlin', O:
Ilk maid and matron hands her dear,
  The baulder that he's hauden, O:
Wi' carcases, claes, blood, an' beer,
  Th' astonish'd floor is laden, O.
      Hartsome is, &c.

Now mak'in peace they ply the grog,
  Tho' strife like haflin's rises, O-
Now party sangs the maist in vogue
  Burst forth frae forty voices, O-
Now sparks, wha scarce dow stagger, try
  To dance to dosin' fiddlers, O-
An' now it dauns, an' hameward hie
  The lasses an' their wheedlers, O.
      Hartsome is, &c.

*An Inn-keeper in Ballycarry.

O village fam't for scenes like thir!
  Sae shelter'd, an sae healthy, O;
Thy sons are firm, thy daughters fair,
  In them, at least, thou'rt wealthy, O:
Till *Isle'magee* surround *Loughmorne,*
  Or yill spring frae the quarry, O,
May plenty, pleasure, peace, adorn
  Carrousin' Ballycarry, O!

      Hartsome is, &c.

GLENO

STRANGER, in Ireland! if your mind
      The bless'd green isle with rapture fills;
As wand'ring o'er her plains, you find
      Grand groves, green lawns, and glassy rills
Descend these bleak and barren hills;
      And soothing contrast, see below,
A village, free from all the ills
      Of Art and Nature - sweet GLENO.

The breezy mount, whose laurels grace
      The winding walk, in flow'rs array'd;
Th' enchanting glen, the sweetest place,
      That Peace and Silence ever stray'd -
The golden glebe, the smooth green mead,
      O'er look'd by lime-cliffs, white as snow -
And gardens fine, that fragrance spread,
      Will charm your heart, that hails GLENO.

Plac'd on the awful precipice,
      That frowns upon the per'lous path;
Oaks, elms and firs, in pomp arise,
      And scorn the shubbery beneath:
The hoarse cascade, august in wrath,
      Ferments the pool, and gliding slow,
Thro' shades, as dark as those of death,
      Salutes the sun beyond GLENO.

Here wealthless Love, by Pride oppos'd,
      In Beauty's ear his hale may hark,
And modest Merit rest, inclos'd
      In safe Retirements holy ark.
The Poet tastefully may mark
      Scenes, fair as fancy e'er could show
And Preacher muse in lab'rinths dark,
      And walk with Wisdom in GLENO.

Sweet village! till thy stable shield
    The everlasting mountains bend;
May Husbandry, completely skill'd
    And Manufacture, thee befriend!
While from yon steep the streams descend,
    That turn thy mills, whose bleachfields glow;
May ample Recompence attend
    On honest Toil, in thee, GLENO

GRACEHILL

THE MORAVIAN SETTLEMENT, NEAR BALLYMENA

Forbear, fierce bigot! why would you inflame
  The torch of zeal, dispensing wounds and death?
How many men, whose faith you rashly blame,
  Do good, seek peace, and walk in wisdom's path?

Come to GRACEHILL, walk up along with me,
  A walk so sweet will cheer your gloomy mind;
Will your cold heart not glow with joy to see
  The little paradise that there you'll find?

Walk round the sylvan scene and fondly view
  The fragrant fruit-tree, and the blossom'd pea;
Herbs of all tastes, and flow'rs of every hue
  Pure as yon Vestal - and as fair as she.

How green these meads! how rich these fields of corn!
  The bean-field blooms, the flax bends to the breeze:
Prolific plenty fills her copious horn,
  And Nature smiles, where Vice and Folly cease.

Compact and clean the mansions that we've pass'd;
  And smooth these Lawns, that milk-white hedges screen:
Tho' not long since, 'twas one wide lonely waste;
  No dome was beauteous, and no lawn was green.

But Culture spoke the word, His friends obey'd;
  The rock they raz'd, th' irriguous marsh they dried
The Genius of the Main uprais'd his head,
  And wonder'd at the changes on his side.

Nor stopp'd he here; the Pow'r who tam'd the waste,
  Went on to regulate the moral frame;
He taught his vot'ries Science, Truth, and Taste,
  And bade 'em pomp and pageantry disclaim.

Here with unerring hand, the Sisters meek
  Their tasteful tasks fulfil. How simply dress'd!
Nor noxious paint distains their modest cheek,
  Nor costly zone adorns their slender waist!

And there, the implements of manual art
  Sound dissonantly, as the Brethren weave;
While health gives sweet Contentment to the heart,
  And Industry forbids pale want to grieve.

Their speech is eloquence; their walk is grace;
  They Piety and Prudence blestly blend:
If this be Heresy, O Prince of Peace!
  Immensely may it spread and never end!

But hark yon bell! it tolls for praise and pray'rs;
  Th' attentive audience in the fane we'll join,
And hear the pealing organ's solemn airs,
  With vocal notes in unison combine.

No silver Shrine is here, nor sculptur'd Bust;
  No pompous Pulpit, nor expensive Pew;
It's builders thought (alas! they're gone to dust!)
  God's noblest temple is a heart that's true -

Adieu! bless'd people; still may care provide
  You competence, and self ne'er tempt to sin!
May Justice ever in your Shop preside,
  And Temp'rance in your hospitable Inn!

And when to earth ye bid a long farewell,
  And dust to dust is reverently giv'n,
May ye hereafter burst th' inclosing cell
  And form a SACRED BROTHERHOOD in Heav'n!

THE GABBON

Thy cliffs, O Gabbon! wild and high,
Appal and please my wond'ring eye:
What rugged ramparts, frowning, fell,
In gloomy grandeur round me swell!

Here, rocks recede; there, lofty peaks:
Projecting shade! romantic creeks!
The steep pile, here, is smooth and even;
There, gash'd in seams, and rudely riven.

Glide on fair ship! beneath us far,
A pigmy seems the trouser'd tar:
The bellowing mound the billows braves,
The hoarse surge thunders in the caves.

A copious cavern in the steep,
Forms a long inroad to the deep;
Yon bark, that glides on waves of glass,
Might up its ample entrance pass.

I have been there, and, under ground,
Explor'd its arch with awe profound;
Ulysses' son thro' such a place
Descending sought the shadw'y race.

High pois'd in air before the cliffs,
The warping wild-fowl pour their griefs:
Close to the shelves their younglings cling,
Where fancy dreads to lift her wing.

Had Fate thought proper to discharge
Some cat'ract vast from Gabbons verge
Th' infracted flood, and raging deep,
Would, mingling, shake this solid steep.

So, fam'd *Ni'gara* from the brink
Of dreadful cliffs is seen to sink;
The furnace foams - the wave recoils -
Th' amazing noise description foils.

Scorn'd by the nymph who charm'd his sight,
The love-lorn Laurence, brave and bright,
From Gabbon's summit, in despair,
Launch'd o'er his form in empty air.

From point to point, down - down he dash'd -
His flesh was torn - his bones were smash'd:
His gore, fast-gushing, ting'd the tide,
The sun, on shore, his cold corpse dried.

Oh! never, never may the strife
Of pride and love and brave men's life,
Till Gabbon firm, in fragments hurl'd,
Fall prostrate 'midst a tottering world!

THE BANKS OF LARNE

ON Larne's sweet banks, in early years,
I careless stray'd, and void of art,
Attun'd a reed that pleased my peers,
To praise the maid that charmed my heart:
A blyther swain rang'd not the green,
And gaudy hills of hapless ERN,
Till spite and malice, chang'd the scene
To grief and care on gentle Larne.

Oft disappointed, oft deceiv'd,
What heart-achs there have marr'd my health!
What humbling insults I've received
From worthless heirs of pride and wealth!
I strove to rise, yet sank the lower;
I sought esteem, and sad concern
From falshood rose; yet all I bore,
While bleast with peace, on gentle Larne.

'Twas there, my heart! a priest-like sire
Impress'd thee with his precepts mild;
There nature's breath, my simple lyre,
Awoke thee soon to warble wild;
There love was selfless and sincere,
There friendship joy'd to watch and warn;
Then is it strange I shed a tear
To leave the gentle banks of Larne?

Inchanting banks! how fair their charms!
The mead adorns, the mountain shields,
On her smooth bosom, cots, flocks, farms,
Reflected, look like fairy-fields:
There villages, and villas rise,
There plenty fills each peasant's barn;
For care, and culture, prompt the wise
To plant, and plow, on gentle Larne.

And must I cease, sweet lake, to view
Thee basking in the tepid ray;
Or tempest-toss'd, and darkly blue;
Or closely veil'd in vapour grey!
Shall I no more, conceal'd by briars,
Eye bathing nymphs, might melt the stern?
Nor mark the meteor of the mires
That nightly glides on gentle Larne?

And must I leave thee, natal cot?
And must thy roof the floor o'erspread?
Alas! my foes, ere long, may blot
My memory on thy ruin'd *stead*:
But welcome shame, and slander's sting,
Th' endanger'd day, the bed of Fern,
Ev'n pain, and death; if these could bring
Repose and peace to gentle Larne.

My comrades kind, these long-lov'd shores,
No more we'll roam on Sundays fine:
Prosperity and peace be yours!
To wander, and to wail, be mine:
You'll sometimes mind a friend, far hence,
Who shares the woes he did not earn,
And pray that fate may recompense
The love he bears to gentle Larne.

ADDRESS TO BELFAST

I have been there and still would go;
'Tis like a little Heav'n below.

WATTS.

FAR-FAM'D Belfast! most justly stil'd
The guide and glory of the North,
Wilt thou attend a songster wild,
Who simply celebrates thy worth?
Tho' prejudice that worth may slight,
Deceiv'd by tales of party-spite,
Story's true page shall carry down
To time's late sons, thy high renown.

Nature, fair-imag'd, walks thy *Stage*,
Thy *Fanes* Morality befriend;
While youths, by Discipline made sage,
Thy throng'd *Academy* attend;
Thy *House of Alms* - asylum bless'd!-
Receives the Poor, and gives 'em rest;
Thy *Sunday-Schools* humanely train
Th' unhappy babes of Want and Pain.

The friends of Liberty and Law,
Brave men and bright, in thee remain;
Whom Demagogue shall nevcr draw
To wild misrule - nor despot chain:
Th' expressive Look - the faultless Form,
Is not thy Daughters only charm;
Good sense, Good-nature, *mental Health*,
Are theirs - a nobler dowr' than Wealth.

While Zeal, elsewhere, directs his Shafts
At the pure Heart that Truth would find;
Free as the gale, that gently wafts
Thy Commerce o'er, thou leavs't the mind:
Thy *Churchman* scorns to smite the meek
and passive *Quaker's* modest cheek:
Thy *Cath'lick* yields her willing hand
To *Calvin's* friend, in Hymen's band.

Ah! ne'er may Ignorance, allied
To Superstition, humble thee!
Nor Opulence engender Pride,
The parent of Misanthropy!
So Emulation shall inflame
Genius to write, that Taste may fame,
And Kindness soothe poor Merit's pains,
And Valour guard what Virtue gains.

Far-fam'd Belfast! O long may stand
Thy domes and spires, that long have stood!
Protected by thy Angel's hand
From Flame, from Tempest, and from flood!
And when old Time, who ruins all,
Shall doom thy splendid streets to fall,
May their exalted Natives rise
To nobler Mansions in thy Skies!

STANZAS

WRITTEN ON THE ISLE OF COPELAND

"This scene had some bold Greek or British bard
Beheld of old, what stories had we heard,
Of fauns, of dryads, and the nymphs their dames,
Their feasts, their revels, and their am' rous flames.-
'Tis still the same, although their airy shape
All but the quick poetic sight escape."

DENHAM

HAIL, Copeland, wild as earthquake's wreck!
    With joy I climb thy shelving side,
That seem'd from far a hoary speck
    Emerging from the circling tide:
    With joy I hear the nymphs, that hide
    In echo's caves, resound my speech;
And see, by Nature's skill supplied
    Smooth pavements round thy ramparts reach.

What fragments huge, at random cast,
    Grotesquely great, bestrew thee round!
What ruins bend, that ev'ry blast
    Seems sent to tumble to the ground!
    Yet fertile grain-fields here abound,
    And fragrant meads, and pastures bland,
For Nature with success has crown'd
    The labours of the lamp-man's hand.

With winding steps, I slowly climb
    Thy beacon, boast of Art's strong hand,
And from its pinnacle sublime,
    With wonder gaze on sea and land:
    Angel of light! here take thy stand,
    And blestly brighten ev'ry ray,
To guide some bark's benighted band,
    That else would perish, long ere day.

While far remov'd from men and guile,
      I enter thus thy grotto grave,
With SHAKESPEARE in "Th' Enchanted Isle,"
      I seem to muse in PROSP'RO's cave.-
      From such a summit SELKIRK brave
      Look'd out for sails from year to year,
And sigh'd for friends beyond the wave,
      In solitude more sad than here:-

For saints of yore might hither fly,
      From persecution's iron rod,
And in thy cells sad requiems sigh
      For martyrs slaughter'd for their GOD:
      And patriot bands, whose bosoms glow'd
      With freedom's holy flame, erewhile,
Might have made this their safe abode,
      Escap'd from tyrants proud and vile.

And here some hermit once might dwell,
      And truth's recipes seek and find;
Though fame no more points out his cell
      Nor where he sleeps, in sea-weeds shrin'd.
      His faithful dog would lick his kind
      Cold, stiff'ning hand, and look and groan;
And he would say - "Thou'rt left behind
      To howl my dirge, and die alone."

Heav'ns! for the prophet's eye who view'd
      Strange visions rise on Patmos' shore,
That here in semblant solitude,
      I might futurity explore;
      And tell wrong'd Europe, drench'd in gore,
      When Pride shall perish, Peace prevail,
And Right, to reign for evermore!-
      But vain the pray'r, and hence we saiI.

Farewell thy tow'r! that long in might
  Immutable shall brave the blast!
Farewell thy cliffs and columns white,
  That ivy-crown'd, seems statues vast!
  Time stole away, and day is past,
  But night is mild, though home be far;-
Yon hill's dark shades our creek o'ercast,
  And Copeland guides us like a star.

ELEGY

WRITTEN IN THE CHURCH-YARD
OF TEMPLECORRAN

Farewell ye cheerful fields! ye blooming plains!
Enough for me the church-yard's lonely mound;
Where melancholy with still silence reigns,
And the rank grass waves o'er the cheerless ground.
                                        BRUCE.

FATIGU'D with toil, yet kept from rest,
        By contemplation, and by care,
I rise and woo the howling East,
        To spend the plaint of grief sincere:
The falling fragment, heard with fear,
        To silence awes the Owls that scream,
While round this long-fallen place of prayer
        I stalk, with spectre-seeming frame.

Hail, hoary structure! wrapt I trace
        The grass-crown'd wall, the weedy pew,
And arches tott'ring to their base,
        And doors on high, that none pass thro';
Craz'd are the cape-stones, once so true,
        Th' unglaz'd, dark holes appal my eye:
The loose pile nods o'er heaps that strew
        Their graves, perhaps, that pil'd them high.

The tile-borne roof, and ponderous beams,
        Dissolved, long since, have chang'd their mode;
Where virgins sung, the cat-club screams,
        And Ruin yawns where Rapture glow'd:
Awe-striking wrecks, where Time has gnaw'd
        Rude bites, and left his cank'rous mark,
On many a slave's long-wish'd abode
        Your frigid shade lies long and dark.

Some soldier here may rest his head,
    Against the breast that brav'd his ball;
Some shepherd join the gentle maid,
    Who frown'd because his flocks were small:
Some never-resting heart of gall
    May melt with his who hated strife -
Oh what a trifle parted all!
    The brittle, frail barrier of life.

How still their hands! how mute their tongues!
    Nor hearts embrace, nor heads invent,
With party toasts, and party songs,
    These trampled roofs are never rent;
No sceptic shocks the senseless saint,
    No fiend of faith stems truth by blows;
In vest of Green the breast is pent,
    Who once the badge of Orange chose.

Pale empress! burst thy sable veil,
    And let me trace thy grave-stones rude:
Why waste the time? what would they tell,
    But some were great - and all were good?
Unnotic'd worth, I know, induc'd
    The nameless dust o'er which I pause,
While to yon shark's sham'd life ensu'd
    The palm of posthumous applause.

Where'er I stray, my footsteps tread
    On some fair maid, and faithful wife;
Some STERNE, whose mirth amuseument spread,
    Or PENN, who mourn'd when rage was rife.
Friends of my dawn, tho' low their life,
    Brave were the hearts whose fall I weep;
Soon shall I leave the scene of strife,
    And in some cell beside them sleep.

The storm shall rise my leaves to spread,
     No fost'ring sun shall raise me higher;
Borne down I droop my friendless head,
     Live on in scorn, and rest require:
So have I seen a trampled briar,
     Whose rustick form could find no prop,
Forbear to fruitlessly aspire,
     And root in earth its simple top

Here, wallowing wild, the reptile hordes
     Shall share the heart whose griefs are vast -
Ah hark, the harsh-ton'd bones and boards!
     Above my bier I hear them cast;
These ashes old, where bless'd with rest,
     The gale-rock'd ravens safely sleep,
Ne'er shed their foliage on a breast
     More pure than his who fills this heap.

His providence with watchful wing
     Screen'd my young life from danger's dart;
I sported in the hamlet's ring,
     While care was his my wants to thwart:
He strove to form my taste and heart,
     My hand he train'd without a rod,
And bade me, void of self and art,
     Befriend my race, and love my God.

Rise Retrospection! gild, re-tread,
     The glimm'ring cells of Mem'ry's cave;
For there stand pictur'd, ne'er to fade,
     The scenes we join'd in, gay and grave:
And let him smile, as when, at eve,
     I chas'd the shower-succeeding arch;
And fire his eye to see the brave
     In self-rais'd ranks beside me march.

And paint his cheek, where care and ease,
    The wrinkle and the rose combine;
And let me hear him, resting raise
    The genial song of love and wine:
And to contrast his converse fine,
    Strike up the harsh and jarring loom:
Th' ennobling fife that leads the line,
    Soft mingling thus, endears the drum.

Yes, drench me, rain! and pierce me, wind!
    And doleful darkness shade me o'er!
Ye can't to me be more unkind,
    Than fate by him was felt before.
Why censure fate? how was he poor
    Whom nature stor'd with honour's pride? -
Or how unschool'd, whose want of lore
    By intuition seem'd supply'd?

Tho' warm, not rash; (his manly mind
    Did adverse attributes contain)
Tho' placid, firm; tho' frugal, kind;
    Tho' deep, not dark; tho' prudent, plain.-
Elate with hope, 'midst friends in pain,
    He reach'd the solemn shore of life,
And in the world-dividing main,
    Bold, launching left the coasts of strife.

The "meek-ey'd morn" divinely wakes:-
    Wrecks, tombs, and trees, once more I mark:
The place of sculls my foot forsakes,
    Reclaim,'d by toil, in shop or park;
But no fond Father's voice I'll hark,
    I had one Friend and here he lies:
His cold clay house is sad and dark,
    But blest repose seals up his eyes.

ADDRESS

TO NOAH DALWAY, OF BELLA-HILL, ESQ

A SELF-TAUGHT bard, who toils his bread to gain,
But toils with pleasure, on a neighb'ring plain,
High-minded DALWAY, thanks you for the praise
(Ill-earn'd, alas!) you gave his woodland lays.
He'd much, much rather one well-judging son
Of genuine taste, would read, and cry- "well done,"
Than want that single smile, and hear the crowd
Salute him as he pass'd with plaudits loud.

Think not encomiums now requests precede;
Nothing I crave, and little do I need;
I've health, content, and labour - mutual friends;
Health breeds content, and labour health amends.
Lone solitude makes all expenses slight,
And how the muse makes solitude delight!
I've learn'd to prize the lot I once decried,
Ere to be poor I reconcil'd my pride.
If proud men scorn my station, what's my care?
I sank not by misdeeds, Fate flung me there;
And, till I shame my life by some base deed,
I'll meet 'em unbash'd, tho' in my humblest weed.

Nor fame, nor fortune, I from verse expect,
Alike undone by beauty and defect;
My rude Scotch rhymes the tasteful justly slight,
The Scotch-tongued rustics scorn each nobler flight;
My mirthful strain makes saints their dull heads shake;
My moral measures can't amuse the rake;
Yet, if a child smile sweet, a poor man smart,
A female charm my breast, a friend depart;
Or a fine landscape meet my raptur'd views,
I'll ne'er, by silence, sin against the muse;
Of independence proud, I'll work and sing,
Poor as a poet, happy as a king.
O might my muse, when she essays to sing,
Above the dogg'rel vale exalt her wing!

[63]

Unsland'ring, uncomplaining, unconfin'd,
Her page the transcript of her vot'ry's mind;
And might a fond few call me, at my end,
A poor, but honest man, who lov'd his friend,
And serv'd him too - I'd, self-approved in heart,
Thank Heav'n for life and death, and peacefully depart.

Hear my warm wish (nor deem me insincere,
The good, in cot or castle, share the pray'r),
May a long life be yours, and its employ
To bless who'er you can, and feel their joy!
May she ne'er know distress, whose form and mind,
Nature made beautiful, and Art refin'd!
May the blest babes whom now you guide and guard
With all the joy of care, your love reward!
Be mild to please, and resolute to dare;
Intrepid as their sire, and as their mother fair!

ADDRESS

*TO MR. A*******, CARRICKFERGUS*

Written after a severe illness

THIS rhyme I sen' to own I'm debtor
To Sandy for his frien'ly letter;
An' certes, had I not grown better
    Before this time,
I wad been makin' scraps o' metre
    In some strange clime.

Twad mak' an humbler body vain,
To think the burial I wad haen:
Sae monie brethren in a train
    Wad gart ye won'er;
But faith! I'm fander to remain
    An' want the honour.

L—d help the Crock wham ailments master,
He meets wi' monie a droll disaster:
Whae'er cam' in prescrib'd some sluister,
    An' I must drink it;
I coupt it up, an' gi'ed a gluister,
    An grue't, an' winket.

This while my sea has been sae rough,
That at your jokes I wadna leugh;
My head was reft wi' ilka cough,
    My breast was strain'd.
Ay when I rav'd, or cry'd och!
    My mither gran'd.

Ay when approch't by lasses lo'esome,
I fand some easement in my bosom,
That cring't wi' fear when carlin's gruesome
    Discours't o' Nick:
Deel rive their jaws! what can dispose 'em
    To scare the sick?

But Sandy, first in my esteem ay,
I'm pleased, an' proud, ye cam' to see me,
Gif folk like you, think something o' me,
                    'Twill never pain me,
Tho' a' the grunters, grave an' gloomy,
                    Quote texts again' me.

Tell that fine chiel wha mens auld watches,
An' him wha doctors crazy clatches,
To see ye a' I'se lift your latches,
                    An' tak' a can,
Whene'er HEALTH men's, wi' braider patches,
                    My inner man.

EPISTLE

TO N— P—, OLDMILL

"The chief musician on the string'd instrument!"

DEAR Thaunie! musick's gentle sinn,
A thread o' rhyme to thee I'll spin;
Tho' unexpressive is your blin'
                An' beamless e'e:
Your brightness has the *light within*
                That pleases me.

I'm glad, my frien', ye mak' a shift
To keep the strings in proper tift;
Ere this new moon forsake the lift
                We'se hae some sport,
Tho' my auld treadles sud move swift,
                At midnight for't.

'Tis you may brag; man, wife, an' lassie,
Wad to their bosoms hug an' hause ye;
Some deep divines, wha poor folk awe sae,
                They flee the kirk,
Wad fald a flock might make them saucie,
                Gif ye were clerk.

Let us be tir'd, or barley-sick,
Or crav'd for debts, wad cowe auld Nick,
Or pierc'd wi' love, aye to the quick,
                Or scandal foutie,
Ae florish o' your fiddle-stick,
                Sen's care to Cloutie.

On auld fair days, when folk's no' sicker,
You're ay the brither o' the Bicker;
Frae ilka neuk the spunkies staucher
                To hear your stories;
The roof re-echoes ev'ry nicher,
                An' every chorus.

An' when ye gravely try your skill
On *ordination* an' *free-will*,
E'en whiggish drones chap in a gill,
              You're sic a bright man;
For a' you're owre like *Rabin Hill*,
              A black New-light-man.

When labour calls, ye doon can lay
Your han's, an' waur the sons o' day;
An' were a wake three mile away
              Ye straught cud gang till't,
An' let them hear ye braith cud pray
              And pit the twang till't.

I 'ledge you're wonderfu' content ay,
An' weel ye may, for fate has sent ye
A bairn-time, thrifty, crouse an' cantie,
              Bless'd be the Maker!
They've bra' stout stilches; tho' they haunt ay
              The "fiddler's acre."

An' sic a wife - but phrase I mannie,
In fegs, I wiss ye saw her *Thaunie!**
My conscience, ye hae graipet cannie,
              While seein' chiels
Wale jads, as gruesome as my grannie,
              Thraun reestet deels.

An' ye hae sense might sair a king,
An' ye've a muse can glibly sing;
Gif I'm to judge, I'll swear by jing!
              There's few wha gaze on
The scenes o' life, can paint the thing
              Like "fine boat-racin."*

* *Thaunie is purblind*
* *Alluding to a song of Thaunie's on a Boat-race*

An' tho' on Nature's bonie beuk,
Ye canna cast a conscious leuk
Ye've *peace* an' *ease*, 'boon monie folk
　　　　　　Wha glour fu' keen,
An' wadna be a cleigh'rin crock
　　　　　　For baith his e'en.

Your case is common; heaps, my frien',
Benight themsel's, wha might hae seen;
Some's *blin* wi' love; some's *blin* wi' spleen;
　　　　　　An some wi' pride;
An' some stap out their *reasons* e'en
　　　　　　That *faith* may guide.

I'd rather than my twa new shoen
I'd view mankin' as ye hae done;
Experience (tho' that camna soon)
　　　　　　Will surely keep
My insight clear, an' save my crown
　　　　　　Till my last sleep.

Hale be your han', to earn a drapie,
By makin' creatures, blythe an' happy!
An' he who peys ye wi' a *rap* ay,
　　　　　　'Cause ye maun trust him,
Let him be Orangeman, or crappie,
　　　　　　I'll say - Deel brust him!

A FRAGMENT

OF AN EPISTLE TO MR. W. H. D.

'Tis no the malice o' the hale,
'Tis no the looms untunefu' peal,
The ragged coat, an' hamely meal,
        That keenly sting;
But something else - I *see* and *feel*,
        But canna sing.

O Nature! cud I set your stage,
Wi' a its scen'ry on my page!
My rainbows points the earth sud guage,
        My wild-fire wander;
An' lakes an' rivers smile and rage,
        Wi' grace an' grandeur.

The purplin' morn, and pensive eve,
Sud a their fine, fair tints receive;
My cliff sud frown, my echo rave,
        My shamrock smell,
My night appear as gran'ly grave
        As night hersel.

My thun'er dreadfully sud soun',
An' still the hum o' hazy noon;
Hill, wood, an' grove, sud (smiling roun')
        Sing, low, and bleat;
An' rough cascades come dashin' down,
        In savage state.

Or cud my manners-paintin' rhymes
"Haud up the mirror" to the times,
I'd sing how *av'rice* gnaws folks wymes,
        How *folly* tipples,
An' how *ambition* thins the climes
        That *love* re-peoples.

The tragedy o' doeless Dodd
Frae shame sud free him if I cud:
Some "village HAMPDENS" patriot blood
              Sud issue, glorous,
Some WOLFE aince mair sud thank his God,
              And die victorious-

I needna strive. My want and woe
Unnerves the energies, you know;
Yet Nature prompts my muse, tho' slow
              An' faints her fires:
The cuckoo sings obscurely low,
              The lark aspires.

Coy science spurn'd me frae her knee,
An' fortune bad my shuttle flee;
But, a' the while, smit strangely wi'
              The love o' sang,
I rudely rhyme the scenes I see,
              Whare'er I gang.

EPISTLE

TO S. THOMSON OF CARNGRANNY

A BROTHER POET

DEAR Thomson! Fav'rite o' the nine!
Wi' wham I shar't the feast of min'
    Before the hag of strife,
Wi' han's that reek't wi' bluid she'd shed,
'Gan wi' the hues o' *black* an' *red*,
    To strip my wab o' life.
Gaun thro' the muir awee ere night
    I mark't *Lyle's* lafty hill;
An' min't the minstrel, blythe an' bright,
    Wha fam't it wi' his quill;
      An' why now, thought I now,
      Hae we been mute sae lang;
      Ise sen' now, an' ken now,
      How things wi' SAMIE gang.

For me, we' a' that's come an' past,
I'm at my ain fire-side at last,
    Fu' blythe, tho' fash't awee,
When geckt at by the purse-proud drove;-
But deel-ma-care, sin' little love
    Is lost 'tween them an' me.
Wi' plackless deels, like us, to board,
    They'd think a burnin' shame,
An' at their revels, tak' my word,
    We'd deem oursel's frae hame:
      While dealin's, an' mailin's,
      They dully egotize on,
      Durst we, Sam, mak' free, Sam,
      To mention rhyme or reason?

L—d! what this pridefu' heart has thol'd
To hear a cuif, whase useless gold
       Ne'er made ae poor man happy,
Expose some selfless son o' worth,
Because half-doil'd wi' wine an' mirth,
       He kent na when to stap ay.
I'd rather drudge, an' do-blacks* roast,
    An' want hale breeks to shift me,
Than shine in ease, gif grubs cud boast
     They lent me gear to lift me.
       We'se debtless, an' fretless,
       Enjoy the mite we hae;
       An' drink whyles, an' think whyles,
       To trifle life away.

I needna fret; the han' o' heav'n
Has gi'en poor me, wham, hardship-driv'n,
       It sav't by lan', an' sea,
A feelin' heart, a thinkin' head,
An' health, an' han's, to win my bread,
       An' comrades firm an' free:
A landscape fine, that charms my e'en
    While workin' sair days-dark on't;
An' Sylvia, an engagin' frien',
     Wha can mak' fine remarks on't:
       Wi' sense grac'd, an mense grac'd,
       An' fand o' truth an' taste,
       While Spring's sweet, she sings sweet,
       She soothes this trampled breast.

* *A kind of potatoe*

Nae wreath shall grace my rustic brows,
But countra folk my dog'rels roose,
      In terms that mak' me blythe;
Tho' whyles scarce worth ae bare babee,
Fancy an' taste, I wadna gie
      For a' Braid-Islan'* tythe.
I'd rather, blest wi' skill an' grace,
      Beg lodgin' in a mill,
Than be the owner o' the place,
      An' want baith taste an' skill.
      Thro' life, frien', my strife, frien',
      Has been to search an' know:
      But slight ay's, the light ay,
      That shines on want an' woe.

But ne'er, tho' pin'd, let's be sae wee
As to implore on supple knee,
      The proud folks patronage;
They ken, fu, brawly whare we stay,
An' gif they notice us they may,
      Aince they've luck't owre our page:
Th' inglorious rhymes o' countra clouns,
      Get plenty to degrade 'em,
Wha wad reward wi' laurel crowns,
      Gif Kings or Priests had made 'em.
      Tho' vain folk disdain folk,
      We'se sing the burns, an' bow'rs,
      O' AIRLAN', our fair lan' -
      Deel tak' *her* faes an' *ours!*

*The Parish of Broad Island

I'll hae to quat my humble strains,
The moon-beams gild my frost-wrought panes,
      An' I've a bit to gang:
I hope your muirlan muse ye'll woo,
To tell me how ye wrastle thro',
      Some time when ye're no thrang.
Atween an' May, gif bowls row right,
    I'll meet ye in *Roughfort,*
An' aince again devote a night
    To frien'liness an' sport.
        Meanwhile, sir, sud bile, sir,
        Mak' factious prose-men fight,
        May leisure, an' pleasure,
        An' peace be ours! - Good night.

ELEGY

ON THE DEATH OF MR. ROBERT BURNS, THE AYRSHIRE POET.

A great man, solely of God Almighty's making such.
                                                          HERON.

The lift begud a storm to brew,
The cloudy sun was vext, an' dark;
A forket flash cam sklentin' thro'
Before a hawk, that chas'd a lark;
Then, as I ran to reach a booth,
I met a swain an' ax't "what news?"
When thus he mourned the far-famed youth
Wha fills the dark, an' narrow hoose.

Sad news! He's gane, wha baith amus'd
The man o' taste, an' taught the rude;
Whase warks hae been mair read an' roos'd
Than onie, save the word o' Gude:
Him genius foster'd on her lap,
An' for his fa' fand fancy mourns;
Dumfries might weel steek ev'ry shap,
An' sen' her tribes to bury Burns.

Oh Burns! oh Burns! the wale o' swains,
Wi' thee the Scottish music fell;
Till nature change, thy artless strains
Shall last, an' seem her second sel:
Was pain thy theme; or pastime daft?
Thou rais'dst the roar, or mov'dst the tear;
Thy "woodnotes wild" were sweet, an' saft,
As grace divine to sauls sincere.

Oh Scotia! Bards of note you've rear'd:
E'en kings were counted i' their train;
But lo! a barefoot moorlun' herd
Frae a' their pipes the praise has ta'en:
What e'er before sae finely felt?
Sae "strongly mark'd" your rustic rings?
What mopin' min' unapt to melt,
Was cauldrife when he swept the strings?

Nae mair wi' rash, repentant share,
He'll breeze the *Daisies* modest breast;
Nor thro' the fur claut here-an'-there
The poor wee *Mousie's* motley nest;
Nae mair, at night, frae toil releas'd,
In "social key" *Scotch Drink* he swiggs;
Nor on a palpitating breast
Is blest amang the *Barley Rigs.*

Nae mair in kirk he stan's tip-tae,
To see the Rooks *ordain* the Raven;
Nor hears his *Cotter* read an' pray,
An' tell the weans the way to heav'n;
But till, unsair't by ear an' e'e,
Auld mem'ry's types ilk image tine,
Wi' a' I hear, and a' I see,
Instinctive thought shall BURNS combine.

Death, wha delay'd, and doff'd his shaft,
An leugh, langsine, to hear his strain,
Has pent him in the cell, which aft
He wiss'd to close him in frae pain:
An' now th' *aerial Wreath* he wears,
Adjudg'd him by the *Phantom Fair,*
An' comes wi' shadowy compeers
To warble on the *Brigs o' Ayr.*

But while the poet we applaud,
We manna less approve the man;
A heart to beauty ay he had,
An' to the brave a frienly han';
Nane felt the love o' country mair,
Nor wiss't the BRETHREN'S peace an' health;
For Independence, firm, an' fair,
He strave as much as fools for wealth.

An' maun his fam'lie i' the slough;
O' dreary poortith, pining, lye?
The want o' him is hard enough,
Without the want o' ought forbye:
Monie fine chiels hae set their hearts,
Like him, owre much on wine an' mirth;
The *failin's* o' a man o' parts
Are nobler than a numscull's *worth*.

In times to come, tho' now obscure,
His line may flourish for his sake;
An' sons o' sang frae monie a shore
Cleave reliques frae his plough or braik:
Sublime, yet simple; wild, yet wise;
He ne'er was match'd wham Scotia mourns -
A noble peal convuls'd the skies,
'Twas Nature's sel' respectin' BURNS.

ELEGY

ON THE DEATH OF HUGH TYNAN

THE POET OF D'DEE

WHILE venal bards, with sordid hand,
      Entwine the wreath for grandeur's brow;
Or pour the dirge, which truth must brand,
      Beside the grave where pride lies low;
I sing an humble child of woe,
      Who daily drain'd the cup of gall -
Happy for those whom hardships bow,
      When they, like TYNAN, early fall.

Ill-fated Tynan! thro' the vale
      Of life, forlorn he crept along,
Culling, at times, with tasteful zeal,
      The sweets of science, and of song:
None prais'd his lay, till mute his tongue,
      None mourn'd his woes, till freed by fate,
How seldom do the thoughtless throng
      Find out poor merit, ere too late?

Oft o'er the page of knowledge bright,
      Or musing sage, he slighted sleep;
And oft, in anguish, veil'd by night,
      He left his cell to "wail and weep":
The man of spirit loves to keep
      His cares conceal'd from cruel pride;
What, what could wound him half so deep,
      As to implore and be denied?

How simply sweet his self-taught strains!
      His life e'en malice cannot blot;
Say men of wealth, who knew his pains,
      Should *famine* fell have been his lot.
While fortune's friend, the tasteless sot,
      In shameful splendor, sins and shines,
Discourag'd, in some lonely cot,
      The man of parts obscurely pines.

[79]

TYNAN! farewell! - I'd rather far
    Possess thy genius, worth, and *cares,*
Than share the proud men's gilded car,
    And have a head, and heart, like theirs:
A short, short while, and doubts and fears
    Shall leave each heart, and tears each eye,
And sad misfortune's honest heirs
    Sing anthems with thy shade, on high.

ELEGY

ON THE DEATH OF HUGH BLAIR, D.D.

DARK midnight reigns; but how can gentle sleep
      (Wildly I cry'd, and wet my couch with tears)
In kind forgetfulness my senses steep,
      Since BLAIR is dead, the pride of modern years?

The venerable Blair, no common priest,
      In life unnotic'd, and unmourn'd in death:
Truth charm'd her scorners in his language dress'd,
      And science smil'd to see him smooth her path.

He no strange system built, nor once put forth
      A dark enigma to a doating head;
The gloomiest sophist on the captious hearth
      Learn'd gentleness and grace from all he said.

But why repine! The hosts of heaven behold,
      The practical and artless TILLOTSON,
And ATTERBURY, masterly and bold,
      Divide their palms with him, who *both* outshone.

Here dy'd away my sympathetic strain,
      Grief sank a while in stupor and in sleep;
But fancy still continued reason's pain,
      Where sad EDINA mourn's her scatter'd sheep.

While fond to hear the far-fam'd foe of vice,
      Amidst his audience pensively I lean'd,
Sedate I saw him in the rostrum rise,
      And heard him say with majesty unfeign'd -

"You I shall teach no more. The prize I reach;
      "But lest you'd wander when my voice should cease,
"I've wrote my precepts that they still may teach
      "An age to come, to follow truth and peace:

"I prov'd them - so must you - discuss - decide -
    "The abus'd apostate whom conviction fires,
"Is nobler than the sots who heir untry'd,
    "Th' implicit faith bequeath'd by senseless sires.

"Knowledge, you've heard me say, may lead to fame;
    "But godlike Virtue up to heaven must lead:
"That *both* were taught you let your lives proclaim,
    "What is the doctrine worth without the deed?

"Refinement and religion, long at strife,
    "I strove to join, and thought the polish'd breast,
"More likely to produce a lovely life,
    "Than the rude soul which no fine art had grac'd.

"Perhaps my lectures may some genius teach
    "To judge aright of beauty and defect,
"And, steep sublimity! thy summit reach,
    "Wild, as e'en OSSIAN, though as POPE correct.

"Perhaps by them, reclaim'd and genuine taste
    "Alike uncouth rusticity shall scorn,
"And affectation, which too long disgrac'd
    "Th' unwieldy page it labor'd to adorn.

"If eloquence by me shall have ally'd
    "Simplicity with pomp, and strength with grace,
"And richly roll'd her elevated tide,
    "The worl'd will pour th' acclaim which once might please.

"But if I've forc'd presumption's tears to flow,
    "Or coax'd young folly into wisdom's yoke,
"Th' unfam'd achievement more consoles me now":
    He said, and ceas'd, and I to care awoke.

ODE TO THE REV. HENRY COOKE, DONEGORE

ON HIS SERMON PREACHED FOR THE BENEFIT
OF THE HOUSE OF INDUSTRY, BELFAST

IF winter wild seem sad and drear,
    To festive bands in mansions bright,
When nightly storms appal the ear,
    And wrecks by day afflict the sight;
        How hapless is their doom who roam
        Without a hope, without a home!
        Who, every rueful day request
        A dole from them whom bread hath bless'd,
        And every weary night a place of rest!

Distress'd they are; but blest their lot,
    Compar'd with such a poorly own
The remnant of a wretched cot,
    And scorn to beg, though work they've none;
        Whose wants, conceal'd by noble pride,
        Because unseen are unsupplied;
        Though, as the grace inhal'd from Heav'n
        Supports the wise to warfare driv'n,
        They'd dearth defy, were some assistance giv'n.

This well you knew, O Christian COOKE!
    As kind in heart, as clear in head,
And when you ably undertook
    The poor house-holder's cause to plead;
        With deep discernment of mankind,
        You mov'd the inmost springs of mind,
        And made Belfast, for ever chief
        In social worth, lend rich relief
        To want-worn Industry, and end his grief.

Whence such supplies? Did Kirwan's shade
    Then actuate thy persuasive tongue?
Or Sterne's soul-swaying pow'r pervade
    The bosoms of the bounteous throng?
        No; 'twas th' AFFLATUS pure, that fir'd
        Isaiah's lips, thy speech inspir'd;
        'Twas Mercy, best-belov'd of Heav'n!
        Descending, made such sums be giv'n
        To toiling Worth, that long with want had striv'n.

As HE, who rest from glory came,
    From death to ransom human-kind,
To health restor'd th' afflicted frame,
    And freed from vice th' ignoble mind;
        So, here, thy audience wisely aim
        To mend the mind, and feed the frame;
        And now, beneath a parent's eye,
        The youth shall read, and labour ply,
        And scape the snares of mean mendicity.

Hail, Charity! whose praise shall last
    When Victory's no longer can:
What's he who conquers empires vast,
    To him who saves one worthy man?
        O! ever thus, in evil days,
        Unnumber'd COOKES to serve thee, raise!
        And may the poor man's ardent prayers,
        For bliss to bands who clos'd his cares,
        From Heav'n descend, on them and on their heirs!

ADDRESS

TO THE REV. WILLIAM GLENDY

*ON HIS BEING ORDAINED PASTOR OF THE
PARISH OF BROAD-ISLAND*

> *"I venerate the man, whose heart is warm
> Whose hands are pure, whose doctrine and whose life
> Coincident, exhibit lucid proof
> That he is honest in the sacred cause."*
>
> COWPER.

THO' rash men from the scorner's chair have hurl'd
    At all the priesthood satire's hissing dart,
Their wild experiments would shew the world
    That, wanting temples, wisdom would depart.

To Wisdom's temple guide, then, good GLENDY!
    Degenerate minds, whom error's toils ensnare;
Denounce the guilty, soothe the suff'rer's sigh;
    Respect the laws, and rev'rence freedom fair.

A sunday-school shall thee as founder hail,
    A reading circle's ruler thou shalt be;
To parts a patron, to diseases pale
    A rare physician, kind without a fee.

Like him thou serv'st, and by his spirit warm'd,
    Who ne'er from doing good supinely ceas'd,
All sects shall share thy friendship; all were form'd
    By one kind sire, and sav'd by one high Priest.

When curs'd "offences come", with prudence sage
    Thou'lt ably arbitrate, and soon restore
Content and kindness to the heart of rage,
    Where prejudice and passion boil'd before.

In times when dearth will wretched want create,
    Shall Charity, the best belov'd of Heav'n,
Descend, and choose thee for her advocate,
    That foes may turn her friends, and much be giv'n.

And thy kind hand shall much to poor men give,
    The heir of wealth thou'lt rouse to tend their cry:
Incautious youth thou'lt teach to wisely live;
    Enfeebled age thou'lt teach to nobly die.

How much can eloquence, sublimely rais'd,
    To truth and goodness all who hear provoke!
Longinus, tho' a Gentile, Moses prais'd,
    And Felix quak'd when Paul of temp'rance spoke.

And thou, a stranger, by thy eloquence
    Hast our free call unanimously gain'd;
"Broad-Island's hope!" cried multitudes immense,
    "Herald of Heav'n - GLENDY we wish ordain'd."

Unmatch'd thy charge; the hero who defends
    The rights of freemen in some injur'd clime,
And sage, who useful arts invents or mends,
    Confer but bounties that must end with time.

But he, whose care converts th' immortal soul,
    Confers a blessing that can know no end,
When yon vast firmament shall, like a scroll,
    Be roll'd away, and Heav'n huge pillars bend.

Then, who dare doctrines pure pervert or hide,
    For lucre's sake, or fame's fallacious breath?
Did Ananias worse? He dross denied,
    Yet him Heav'n sentenc'd to immediate death.

Proceed then, conscious of th' important trust,
    T'enforce our duties, thus fulfilling thine:-
To life's best book - to principle, be just,
    And by example let thy precepts shine.

When God's grand trump from Heav'n to Hell shall ring,
 And worlds, all aw'd, attend its deep-ton'd voice,
May we, with thee, uprais'd on rapture's wing,
 String harps of gold, and round the throne rejoice.

And may Broad-Island's fane, in which of old
 The first Dissenter preach'd on Erin's plain,
For faithful teachers be through time extoll'd,
 And congregations free from falsehood's stain!

THE PENITENT

INSCRIBED TO THE REV J BANKHEAD

WRITTEN IN THE YEAR 1800

Not all the pride of empire,
Ere gave such blest sensations, as one hour
Of PENITENCE, tho' painful.
                                              BROOKE

EARTH feels the triple scourge wild warfare spreads,
    Emaciate *famine* gnaws the husks and pines,
And ev'ry friend, forsaking, inly dreads
    The fated wretch, whom *pestilence* confines:-
Say, will BANKHEAD, who piously declines
    Man's ev'ry vice, and mourns his woes severe;
Will he, the guide, who feels what he enjoins,
    The fervent love of ev'ry *faith* and *sphere,*
The Penitent's memoirs, tho' mean, be pleas'd to hear?

His name, if I min' right, was *Christy Blair.*
    Fu' aft I've pass'd the wa'-stead whare he leev'd;
An' auld ash tree stan's branchless now an' bare,
    Aboon the spring, unnotic'd an' unpreev'd:
The side wa' co'ers the causey that he pav'd,
    The beasts rub doon the cheeks o' ilka door;
Rank nettles hide the hearth on which he shav'd
    The nybers ance a week in years o' yore -
I learn'd his life frae *Brice,* the auld herd on the moor.

He weav'd himsel', an' keepet twathree gaun,
    Wha prais'd him ay for hale weel-handled yarn;
His thrifty wife an' wise wee lasses span,
    While warps and queels employ'd anither bairn;
Some stript ilk morn an' thresh'd, the time to earn
    To scamper wi' the houn's frae hill to hill;
Some learn'd the question-beuk in nyb'ring barn -
    Christy wrought unco close, whyles took a gill,
But when his wab was out had ay a hearty fill.

An' nae mean spunge was he; but was hae lent
    Sums to poor sots, wha basely brak their word;
Rich rakes admir'd his sprie, sae weel he kent
    The way to heel, an' han', a guid game bird:
An' in the pit he wadna twice be dar'd,
    The odds were shamefu' when he cried "fair play";
His nieve, that nail'd the messons to the sward,
    Wad stapt to lift their weanies frae his way:
He harm'd himsel' at times was a' that folk cud say.

But och! if vice the least indulgence claim
    'Twill wax, an' strengthen, like a wean at nurse;
Belyve he staid hale days an' nights frae hame,
    Tho' ae nights absence, ance he deem'd a curse;
An' aft brought hame nought but an empty purse,
    O' a' the hale wabs price he took to sell;
Then, sick niest day, poor Mary boost disburse
    Her pence, to get a glass his qualms to quell:
She grudg'd - he storm'd - the weans grat - hame grew hell.

At length he turn'd a doonright ne'er-do-weel,
    For ilka draught, he swore, but made him dryer;
The kye gaed baith for debt. A sorry chiel'
    Was he to cleave their stakes to men' the fire:
Mary ne'er min't the house - mair like a byre,
    But clash'd wi' nyber wives. Unkent to him
For tea, an' snuff, the troubled dame's desire,
    She'd smuggled meal an' seeds; tho' hunger grim
Devour'd the duddy weans, now in a wretched trim.

Gif ye had pass'd his door, ye'd either heard
    Him we his comrades madly makin' noise,
Or squabblin' wi' the wife. He seldom car'd
    To wake the looms mair profitable voice:
The weans were wicked mair thro' chance than choice
    How marvellous wad been their mense an' grace!
He learn'd the lasses smut, an' gart the boys
    Drink dreadfu' toasts, an' box for pence or praise;
They'd ca' their mother le'er, an' curse her till her face.

Whyles wi' his auld colleagues he blam'd his wife;
  He kent that she was slack, an' they were fause:
She sometimes took a drap, an' by the life
  A drinkin' wife's ay deem'd for greater flaws:
Ance when they differ'd, like a thoughtless ass,
  He listed wi' the sogers on the street,
Yet when he ru'd, wrang'd Mary pledg'd her braws
  To raise the smart money. To see her greet
Wad thow'd the hardest heart in army or in fleet.

Yet shame owrecam' him whyles, an' when advice
  Was properly applied it rous'd his pride,
He'd kiss the beuk, an' swear by a' the skies,
  He'd *in nae change house* drink till hallon-tide;
Then, then he thrave; but och! he cudna bide
  Frae worthless spen'thrifts, nor cud they frae him;
At first he'd drink his glass in some backside,
  But at the table when his brains 'gan swim;
When tald o' a' niest morn he'd tremble ev'ry limb.

At lang an' last, when to the frightfu' edge
  O' dreary ruin, by his courses brought,
(For a' was gaen he had to sell or pledge
  The times were hard and nane would trust him ought)
To pass a painfu' hour, the barn he sought
  Whare Smyth, the methodie, harangu'd the folk:
They mourn'd, an' cried amen - he fleech'd and fought,
  Christy grew grave, an' thought he'd join the flock,
An' imitate their lives wham ance he us'd to mock.

An' change his life he did; the bull-beat came,
  He wadna gang; but ca'd it savage vice:
A serious nyber 'cause he stay'd at hame
  Gi'ed him a wab to weave, an' lent the price:
Late, late did he sit up, an' early rise,
  An' eat the bread o' care to get it weav'd;
Syne took it hame, gat meal, an' monie nice
  Auld claes, to thack the weans, we thanks receiv'd;
Somebody ay will help the poor an' weel-behav'd.

Nature a while, tho' thought forbearance hard,
      An' Habit, like a bough by force held straight,
Sprang till its ain auld thraw. When aff his guard,
      Twathree rash gills wad set him till't a' night;
An' much he'd said an' done that was na right:-
      Ilk short relapse the clashes met to track o';
But practice soon made irksome trials light;
      As ane, at first, wha trys the pipe for lack o'
His health, halts, coughs, an' greus, yet *learns* to like tobacco.

While perseverin' in his heav'n-ward way,
      He lea's pale want behin', his cant' an' zeal,
Sae quite remarkable, mak' grave an' gay
      Laugh hearty at him, tho' they like him weel;
Has he a band to fill? he soon fin's bail,
      Nae pross ere plagues him now, sloth leas his hame;
He has baith kye an' corn, an' sells some meal,
      His frien's outbye add *mister* till his name;
An' alter'd Mary's now a douse an' dainty dame.

(Hail! good old WESLEY - this they owe to thee,
      The wise of all professions bless thy birth;
Believing what you taught, without a fee,
      "A poor way-faring man," you ventur'd forth,
Striving where'er you went to free the earth
      From sin, enslaver of the human mind:-
As godlike HOWARD, friend of woe an' worth,
      In many a realm consol'd the cells where pin'd
Poor persecuted slaves, kept there by kings unkind.)

Whase arm ance rash as Christy's? now tho' strong,
      Nae bangster tholes his nieve or sla-thorn black;
Wha ance blasphem'd like Christy? now his tongue
      Without minc'd oaths the lee-lang day can crack:
His nights ance spent with gamesters owre the pack
      Are pass't wi' deein' wights, or at his beuk;
The lyin' cash he ance wad sent to wrack,
      Lent, int'rest-free, sets up new-married folk -
He's far owre wise to jibe; but no owre grave to joke.

The weans and Mary kept the cottage neat;
    She was affectionate, an' fond were they;
They work't an' sang their hymns, and crack't, an' gree't,
    Fine was their speech, an' affable their way.
They werena stupes, wha fient na word can say
    For what they b'lieve; tho' first to rail an' rage
At a' wha differ. 'Mang some bolefu's mae,
    Ane *Fletcher's* warks, a bra unbias'd sage,
Gart' em wi' might an' mense the Calvinists engage.

An' searchin' for the Truth improv'd their taste:
    How nat'ral *Joseph's* Life was weel they kent;
How *Moses'* muse her notes sublimely rais'd,
    An' *Jeremiah's* deeply did lament;
The *spen' thrift son's* fine scene they weel cud paint,
    An guid *Samaritan's* - an' nearer han',
How *Young* made night mair solemn wi' his plaint;
    How *Milton's* eve was fair, his Adam fand;
How *Gray* was sad an' grave, an' *Shakespeare* wildly grand.

They min't baith warls. In warps boil'd by their han'
    Did thrice ten shuttles lose their entrails sma';
An' on a scoup o' cheap, but mountain lan',
    They graz'd yell kye, an' drain'd, an' lim'd the shaw.
Beasts, yarn, an' claith, aft call'd the sons awa';
    The daughters wash'd, an' sew'd, an' span wi' care:
Christy did little, but directed a';
    An' cute was he when unco folk were there;
For at the very warst he had baith sense an' lear.

"The e'e that saw them bless'd them." Much they shar'd
    Wi' frien's, wi' strangers', an' wi' a' in need;
Folk thought the fam'ly *fey* if e'er they err'd,
    Bonnier an' better ne'er brak warls bread:
Christy ne'er strave to cross their loves; but gied
    Mailin's, an' gear, to ev'ry lad an' lass,
He leev'd to train their weans, an' when he died,
    Was what they ca' the leader o' a class -
Brice gied me this account, an' right weel pleas'd I was.

May my wild brethren turn to wisdom's path
      An' grace poor Erin, plagu'd with want and dearth!
And banish from her shores religious wrath,
      Desponding sloth, and dissipated mirth!
May sun-like Science from the poor man's hearth
      Chase Ignorance, the owl that haunts the stys!
So patriots brave, when we lie low in earth,
      "Harmless as doves, and yet as serpents wise,"
Shall follow Truth and Right, and guard the land they prize.

THE PRIEST'S ANTHEM

Tune - "Plato's Advice"

SINCE rev'rend brothers just and good,
     Who've, with a faith that will not fade,
The solemn covenant renew'd,
     You oft before us Christians made:
Should not a vigil now be given
     To serious song, and converse rare?
Shall souls sustain'd with food from Heav'n
     Like worldly minds be crush'd with care?

'Tis not the red cross that we wear,
     'Tis not the crosier that we wield,
Nor vestments white, nor mitres clear,
     On which our bands distinction build.
But that with ev'ry fiend we war,
     With God's support, and overcome;
Conducted by the cloudless star,
     Of Hope divine to Heavenly home.

While Levites false, who tithe the earth,
     And starve the flocks they vow'd to feed,
Are scorn'd, as people not in worth
     Peculiar, but in pride and greed:
We hold the volume in our hands
     Whose word was sent the heart to purge;
And practising its pure commands,
     Adorn the doctrines that we urge.

The slaves of guilt, if wisdom's lamp
    Their desp'rate state would let them see,
Might rise as from a dungeon damp,
    To life, and peace, and liberty:
They'd soon withdraw, in holy haste,
    From worthless brethren, sons of strife;
And at our altars richly feast,
    And fondly quaff the streams of life.

Now part in peace; and may the band
    Its glorified High Priest adore
In New Jerus'lem, that shall stand
    When time's whole works shall be no more.
And O! with us, may all the lodge
    Whom we're ordain'd to guide and guard,
Be blest by Heav'n's impartial judge,
    With vict'ry's palm, a rich reward.

THE DYING MASON

Tune -"Lochaber."

FAREWELL to the village, the best on the plain,
The lough, glen, an' gran' hill, I'll ne'er see again;
Adieu to my pleasure! adieu to my care!
My poor auld frail folk, an' my lassie sae fair:
The kirk whare I promis'd wi' folly to part,
An' the inn that ensnar'd me I lea without smart;
But och! how the sons o' the Lodge can I lea,
An' gae to my lang hame - the cauld house o' clay?

Nae mair shall I gang, while in this side o' time,
A step nearer light in the order sublime;
Nae mair, while ilk mouth's clos'd, an' fast the door bar'd,
Initiate the novice, baith curious and scaur'd;
Nae mair join wi' scores in the grand chorus saft,
Nor fandly toast "Airlan' - an' peace to the craft":
I ay cud been wi' ye, but now I maun stay
Confin'd in my lang hame - the cauld house o' clay.

Sin' I was a Mason a sad life I had;
The cauld cantin' crew everlastingly gnaw'd;
That I "met the Deel in the Lodge ay," they said,
They maun men' if they miss him, ere a' plays be play'd:
If Cowan an' Craft fand me punctually just,
No blabbin' a secret, nor triflin' wi' trust,
My place may be higher than folk's wha mair pray,
When rais'd frae my lang hame - the cauld house o' clay.

THE CRAFTSMEN OF BALLYCARRY

Tune - "Free and Accepted Mason."

KIND visiting stranger, who roams without danger
    Through Erin, the land we love dearly;
Since you've passed the best judge that belongs to our lodge,
    You're a worthy, and welcome sincerely.

Your health and your number, shall wake echo's slumber,
    Nor shall you sleep long while you tarry,
For the rafters shall ring, with a song that we'll sing,
    On the craftsmen of sweet Ballycarry.

The coin that our labour brings in from our neighbour,
    (Kind offices duly fulfilling,)
In moments of leisure, though temp'rate, with pleasure,
    We socially sport off a shilling.

If some pilgrim old should his hardship unfold,
    With a glass and a guinea we'll cheer him;
And the child unprotected, if to us directed,
    We'll bless brother's orphan, and rear him.

Though blund'rers from Babel, an ignorant rabble,
    Oppose us with raging and violence,
Removing their blindness, to brotherly kindness,
    Our conduct shall shame them to silence.

Mayn't our maxims be good, though some false brethren rude
    Break through laws they profess to put faith in?
For the multitude found by the Christian creed bound,
    Live far worse than Jew, Turk, or Heathen.

Were our myst'ry declar'd, the most proud would knock hard
    At our door and implore to be aided,
For Fox's great heart, kneeling down, kiss'd our art,
    And our arch mighty NELSON o'ershaded.

Since the brave and the wise would our order despise,
    If it stood on a sandy foundation;
The warrant and shield make encampments well fill'd,
    With fidelity, peace, and compassion.

We'll join in a ring, the craft and the King
    We'll honour with bumpers o'erflowing,
May the *Grand Lodge* of worth, the *Pole-star* of the North,
    From its pure light never cease glowing!

While our Templars range through lands native and strange,
    Adversity's storms may they weather;
May Masonry's dove o'er the universe move,
    And ne'er of her wing lose a feather.

ADDRESS

SPOKEN IN ST PATRICK'S LODGE, CARRICKFERGUS, ON ST PATRICK'S DAY, 1808

SHALL pride or scorn debase the mind,
    Loose mirth, dull care, or rude debate,
While here we're met, compatriots kind!
    In social peace to celebrate
The sainted Sage, whom to our state,
    To GOD she serves, in kindness gave,
To publish truth, and cultivate
    Our fam'd forefathers, wildly brave.

He wav'd Religion's hallow'd wand;
    The red-cross rais'd on ev'ry shore;
And Error's snakes forsook the land,
    And Vice's wolves were fierce no more.
The fountains that be blest, have pow'r,
    The pilgrim deems, to cure his frame,
And venerates the ruins hoar
    Of temples old; that bear his name.

And long the tribes he came to bless
    Would have observ'd his precepts sage;
Had not, insuring sad success,
    Base conquest bade division rage.
Alas! thro' many a barb'rous age,
    Did sect with sect, and clan with clan,
Disgrace our hist'ry's hideous page,
    Renouncing the reformer's plan.

Till sun-like Reason, clear and warm,
      To gild the mental gloom awoke;
And strong Delusion's wizard charm
      By her celestial influence broke;
And Equity arose and spoke
      In senates liberal, just, and wise;
And Candor's converts burst the yoke
      Of visionary Prejudice.

Nor shall there one complaint remain,
      For GRATTAN will befriend FINGAL;
And all an equal right shall gain
      T' attend their common country's call.
Then should th' invader, to enthrall
      These sea-sav'd shores, his legion's arm,
ERIN's whole race, a living wall
      Shall round her constitution form.

While to our Patron's memory
      With heart and voice we homage pay,
If he beholds us, hov'ring nigh,
      What joy his rev'rend locks display;
That, on the shore he wont to stray,
      His filial sons, a friendly train,
Engage thus firmly to obey
      His dictates pure, that sots disdain.

Yes, by his sprite inspir'd, we swear
      "Good-will to man," and mutual peace,
Nor, for opinion's sake, will e'er
      The man of principle disgrace;
And never may a bosom base
      Our emblematic Shamrock wear,
Nor dastard, deaf to ERIN's praise,
      Her heaven-strung harp with rapture hear!

But health to ERIN's patriot bands,
 (Whether her plains they proudly stray,
Or gain her praise in distant lands),
 Conven'd to keep this holy day!
Ev'n now, with us, I hear 'em say,
 As to acclaim, they ready stand,
May worth, peace, freedom, ever sway,
 The Isle of Saints, and heroes grand!

SONG

Tune - "When bidden to the Wake or Fair."

COME let us here, my Brethren dear,
    Secluded thus from vulgar sight,
In Fellowship and Friendship rear
    A Temple up to Love and Light:
On Truth's firm ground its walls we'll found;
    Our Union shall cement it sure;
Strife's hammer's rash, shall never clash
    Against the Lodge of Ballynure.

Proud party, wrath, nor forms of faith,
    Shall ne'er divide hearts try'd and true;
Heads that are wise, we'll ne'er despise,
    Whether they choose to crop or queue:
The good of ev'ry creed and clime,
    Calvinian, Cath'lick, Manx, or Moor,
Shall be accepted, any time,
    By us, the Lodge of Ballynure.

Unlike the band that blasts our land,
    And serves Division's hell-hatch'd fiend,
We'll practise peace, and coalesce
    With amity and order's friend:
Not torture's rack shall us affright,
    Nor tempting promises allure,
To violate the *Rules of Right,*
    And shame the Lodge of Ballynure.

The *Widow's* shield, the *Olphan's* stay,
　　The *Stranger's* guide we'll ever be;
Sweet *Innocence* we'll ne'er betray,
　　Nor to *Injustice* bend our knee.
Yes, nymphs divine, you'll find us just,
　　Tho' priestly shackles don't secure;
They'll find much truth, who much dare trust
　　Pure honour's Lodge in Ballynure.

We'll live by Rule, and void of Pride,
　　Alike and Level, meet and part:
Prudence shall o'er our lips preside,
　　And Charity expand our heart:
Silence, within, the Craft shall 'spy,
　　And Secrecy shall tile the door:
On Worth and Wisdom's pillars high
　　We'll *raise* the Lodge in Ballynure.

When far-fam'd cities, "cloud-capt towers,"
　　And time-worn temples, grave and gray -
When all these mighty works of ours,
　　And earth itself shall pass away,
May Nature's Builder, he who bids
　　Heaven's lights blaze out, or be obscure,
Preside on high with sleepless lids,
　　O'er us, the Lodge of Ballynure.

ST JOHN'S DAY

Tune - "Langolee."

Our brethren approach, we'll move forward to meet them,
    The banner unfurl and let mild music play;
Their ranks open wide, now with honour we'll greet them,
    Whose emblems of office their orders array:
Beneath the high arch of the firmament spacious,
Let deacons distribute the love-feast so gracious;
And "health to the king, peace to Erin thrice precious,
    And Heav'n to the craft," let the brotherhood say.

At high twelve to the temple we walk in procession,
    To hear virtue taught from the book of the law;
Here charity's sweets make a wond'rous impression
    On kind cordial hearts, that grand wisdom must awe:
But hark! how our guide ends the best of orations!-
"Love the lodge, but much more, love all sects in all nations!
And may masonry's morals, in glorious gradations,
    Refine isles as rude as the sun ever saw!"

'Tis done, and the visiters homeward now filing,
    Salute each blythe band as it passes them by;
Each, decently mute, looks a fond farewell smiling,
    While friendship in heart brightens joy in his eye:
Where a maid deigns to smile, how her lover's heart's glowing!
Where a dame meets her mate, what applause she's bestowing!
Each boy cries "such vestments shall round me be flowing
    If ripe years of manhood I reach ere I die."

Want's children, this day, by collections quite ample,
  Gain'd sums that may serve them till dearth is no more;
What crowds curiosity lured to the temple,
  Who seldom there hail'd Heaven builder before!
This day to the poor man's bruis'd bosom imparted
An hour's proud importance; on it the warm-hearted,
Fond genius of friendship her influence exerted,
  And forc'd party spirit from blest Erin's shore.

How right are our rules! cast on earth's rudest region,
  A mason finds friends though they know not his speech;
The pris'ner of war scapes the woes of his legion,
  If fellowship's right hand he fitly can reach.
From Heav'n, men of Ulster! (who bounteously yielding
To sympathy's summons, are poor orphans shielding,)
Shall mercy descend to the mansion you're building,
  Where want she'll alleviate, and ignorance teach.

Then, prejudice cease! O, if o'er the wide world
  Our pure rules were practised, what justice would be!
The flags of all tyrants for aye would be furl'd,
  They'd call their slaves brethren and soon set them free;
"Peace on earth and good-will," would end war, man-destroying,
The humblest alive, his whole heart's wish enjoying,
Would see the tam'd wolf with the playful lamb toying,
  From under his rich vine, or fruitful fig-tree!

THE IRISHMAN

Tune - "Vive la."

THE savage loves his native shore,
  Though rude the soil and chill the air;
Well then may Erin's sons adore
  Their isle, which Nature formed so fair!
What flood reflects a shore so sweet,
  As Shannon great, or past'ral Bann?
Or who a friend or foe can meet,
  So gen'rous as an Irishman?

His hand is rash, his heart is warm,
  But principle is still his guide -
None more regrets a deed of harm,
  And none forgives with nobler pride.
He may be duped, but won't be dared;-
  Fitter to practise than to plan,
He dearly earns his poor reward,
  And spends it like an Irishman.

If strange or poor, for you he'll pay,
  And guide to where you safe may be;
If you're his guest, while e'er you stay,
  His cottage holds a jubilee:
His inmost soul he will unlock,
  And if he should *your* secrets scan,
Your confidence he scorns to mock,
  For faithful is an Irishman.

By honour bound in woe or weal,
  Whate'er she bids he dares to do;
Tempt him with bribes - they won't prevail,
  Try him in fire, you'll find him true.
He seeks not safety: let his post
  Be where it ought, in danger's van:
And if the field of fame be lost,
  'Twill not be by an Irishman.

Erin, loved land! from age to age,
  Be thou more great, more fam'd and free!
May peace be thine, or, should'st thou wage
  Defensive war, cheap victory!
May plenty bloom in every field;
  Which gentle breezes softly fan,
And cheerful smiles serenely gild,
  The home of every Irishman!

THE EXECUTION

AWAKE my lire, and sing his fall
     Who on yon tree must yield his breath:
Nor censure me, you hearts of gall;
     I blame his deeds, but mourn his death.

The bosoms that fine feelings bless,
     Must grieve to see an erring swain,
Ascend the climax of distress,
     Disgrace, remorse, affliction, pain.

The warlike guard, the sable priest,
     The false-fac'd fiend, and warping mob,
That scare the safe, must shock the breast
     Which long ere night shall cease to throb.

The deep damp cell in twilight furl'd,
     The filth that rots, the bolt that galls,
He's griev'd to leave; and with a world
     Would buy a week within these walls.

Ah! see him led to life's last scene
     Thro' Carrickfergus' far-fam'd wall;
Whose mart is copious, fair her fane,
     Her fortress firm, and just her hall.

Amid the circle see him bend
     His neck, now bare, the noose to meet:
And now the steps he'll ne'er descend,
     He climbs with loth and lingering feet.

Where shall he turn? His actions here
    A woeful retrospect supply;
Confronting what a dark and drear
    Hereafter, shocks his mental eye!

Heaven's azure arch he dreads to scan,
    Heaven's easy laws he held in strife,
With shame he views the cruel clan
    Intent to see him lose his life.

Where e'er he looks his heart must bleed;
    He sees the ruffian who betrayed;
He sees th' accomplice of the deed;
    He sees his friends and favourite maid.

He sees his father. Torments move
    His inmost soul, as near he draws:
To see them grieve whom much we love
    Is death. 'Tis worse when we're the cause.

His last address had power to reach
    Ev'n scornful hearts, tho' void of art:
Affecting still must be the speech
    That simply leaves a feeling heart.

The choral psalm with sad delight
    Consol'd the breasts his speech had riv'n,
To hear him sing an angel might
    Lean from the battlements of heaven.

In plaintive and pathetic strains,
    To Beings source he wills his soul;
A long last gaze o'er hills and plains
    His sad eyes take, and cease to roll.

He hesitates, and looks again
    Then veils the cheek where blooms the rose,
His pendent form with pungent pain
    Convulsive writhes, and wildly throes.

Heav'ns! see him struggle, spring, and stretch
    Now swell, now sink, now scarcely shake
So, on the hook, the finny wretch
    Hangs trembling o'er its parent lake.

ELEGY

COMPOSED BY NIGHT, UNDER THE GALLOWS

On Knockagh's cliffs, the night-gale loudly roars,
    The streamlet shines beneath the moon-beam wan;
The breaking surges lash the lonely shores,
    Unseen, unheard, by rest-partaking man:

While here I rest beneath the Gallow's tree,
    Plac'd on the grave where rots some felon vile;
And ponder on the guilt and misery
    Of convicts, punish'd on this gloomy pile.

Here has expir'd the Rake, who meanly bar'd,
    The bleach-field fine, or pilfer'd in a shop;
And Rapine's bolder son, who sternly dar'd
    To burst the mansion, or the chaise to stop.

Here too, th' Assassin hung, who, false in wrath,
    Plung'd his keen dagger in his comrade's side;
And monstrous Hag, who harshly put to death
    Th' offenceless babe, whose birth she hop'd to hide.

For crimes of ev'ry kind, men of all creeds,
    Have suffer'd here, 'mid multitudes who mourn'd;
Some had their hearts cut out, some lost their heads,
    And some, half strangl'd, in a tar-tierce burn'd.

Vast torments were their due, and vast were giv'n;
    But Innocence! was e'er thy blood here spilt?
Did'st thou, cast off by men, appeal to Heav'n,
    And to thy latest breath deny thy guilt?

May HE, whose earthquake shook the pillar'd gate,
  And burst the cell to set the pris'ner's free,
Hurl down his vengence, ere it be too late,
On the false foe of wrong'd INTEGRITY!

A PRAYER

Written on the eve of the unfortunate 7th of June, 1798

ALMIGHTY Lord of life and death!
     While men for strife prepare,
Let but this heart thy favour feel,
     And peace will still be there.

How oft I've err'd! at pleasure's shrine
     How fondly bent my knee!
But if I have not cruel been,
     Be clement, Lord! to me.

If pride in this aspiring breast
     Made poverty give pain,
Expel that pride; nor in its stead
     Let mean dishonour reign.

If e'er ill passions prompted me
     Off wisdom's path to go,
Let not revenge, the worst one, strive
     To hurt a private foe.

How dare I ask thy bolts to throw?
     Whose mandate's "do not kill."
But, whilst as man I have to fight,
     As man O may I feel!

Let not this frame, whose fleshless bones
     These summer suns may bleach,
Lie writhing long; nor, while it stands,
     The hand of pillage stretch.

But in the vict'ry, or the rout,
    In glory, or in gall,
May moderation mark my power,
    And fortitude my fall.

Why dread to die? what griefs I've borne?
    What pains have pluck'd each nerve?
Yet why not wish to grow more wise,
    And live my friends to serve?

Resign'd I'll rest then, whether oft
    Yon silver curve to see;
Or hail the sun, and, ere he set,
    Beyond his system be.

Almighty Lord of life and death!
    Whilst men for strife prepare,
Let but this heart thy favour feel,
    And peace will still be there.

DONEGORE HILL

Ephie's base bairntime, trail-pike brood,
Were arm'd as weel as tribes that stood;
Yet on the battle ilka cauf
Turn'd his backside, an' scamper'd aff.

PSALM 78, v.9.

The dew-draps wat the fiels o' braird,
That soon the war-horse thortur'd;
An falds were op'd by monie a herd
Wha lang ere night lay tortur'd;
Whan chiels wha grudg'd to be sae tax'd
An tyth'd by rack-rent blauth'ry,
Turn'd out *en masse*, as soon as ax'd -
An unco throuither squath'ry
      Were we, that day.

While close-leagu'd crappies rais'd the hoards
O' pikes, pike-shafts, forks, firelocks,
Some melted lead - some saw'd deal-boards -
Some hade, like hens in byre-neuks:
Wives baket bonnocks for their men,
Wi' tears instead o' water;
An' lasses made cockades o' green
For chaps wha us'd to flatter
      Their pride ilk day.

A brave man firmly leain' hame
I ay was proud to think on;
The wife-obeyin' son o' shame
Wi' kindlin e'e I blink on:
"Peace, peace be wi' ye! - ah! return
Ere lang and lea the daft anes" -
"Please guid," quo he, "before the morn
In spite o' a' our chieftains,
      An' guards, this day."

But when the pokes o' provender
Were slung on ilka shou'der,
Hags, wha to henpeck didna spare,
Loot out the yells the louder.-
Had they, whan blood about their heart
Cauld fear made cake, an' crudle,
Ta'en twa rash gills frae Herdman's* quart,
'Twad rous'd the calm, slow puddle
                              I' their veins that day.

Now *Leaders*, laith to lea the rigs
Whase leash they fear'd was broken
An' *Privates*, cursin' purse-proud prigs,
Wha brought 'em balls to sloken;
Repentant Painites at their pray'rs,
An' dastards crousely craikin',
Move on, heroic, to the wars
They meant na to partake in,
                              By night, or day.

Some fastin' yet, now strave to eat
The piece, that butter yellow'd;
An' some, in flocks, drank out cream crocks,
That wives but little valu'd:
Some lettin' on their burn to mak',
The rear-guard, goadin', hasten'd;
Some hunk'rin' at a lee dyke back,
Boost houghel on, ere fasten'd
                              Their breeks, that day.

*An Innkeeper in Ballycarry

The truly brave, as journeyin' on
They pass by *weans* an' *mithers*,
Think on red fiel's, whare soon may groan,
The *husbands*, an' the *fathers*:
They think how soon thae bonie things
May lose the youths they're true to;
An' see the rabble, strife ay brings,
Ravage their mansions, new to
                    Sic scenes, that day.

When to the tap o' DONEGORE
Braid-islan' corps cam' postin',
The red-wud, warpin, wild uproar,
Was like a bee scap castin';
For ******* ***** took ragweed farms,
(Fears e'e has ay the jaundice)
For *Nugent's* red-coats, bright in arms,
An' rush! the pale-fac'd randies
                    Took leg, that day.

The *camp's* brak up. Owre braes, an' bogs,
The *patriots* seek their *sections*;
Arms, ammunition, bread-bags, brogues,
Lye skail'd in a' directions:
Ane half, alas! wad fear'd to face
Auld Fogies, faps, or women;
Tho' strong, untried, they swore in pride,
"Moilie wad dunch the yeomen,"
                    Some wiss'd-for day.

Come back, ye dastards! - Can ye ought
Except at your returnin',
But wives an' weans stript, cattle hought,
An' cots, an' claughin's burnin'?
Na, haste ye hame; ye ken ye'll 'scape,
'Cause *martial worth* ye're clear o';
The nine-tail'd cat, or choakin' rape,
Is maistly for some hero,
                                     On sic a day.

Saunt Paul (auld Knacksie!) counsels weel -
Pope, somewhere, does the samen,
That, "first o' a', folk sud themsel's
Impartially examine;"
Gif that's na done, whate'er ilk loun
May swear to, never swith'rin',
In ev'ry pinch, he'll basely flinch -
"Guidbye to ye, my brethren."
                                     He'll cry, that day.

The leuks o' wheens wha stay'd behin',
Were mark'd by monie a passion;
By dread to staun, by shame to rin,
By scorn an' consternation:
Wi' spite they curse, wi' grief they pray,
Now move, now pause a bit ay;
"Tis mad to gang, 'tis death to stay,"
An unco dolefu' ditty,
                                     On sic a day.

What joy at hame our entrance gave!
"Guid God! is't you? fair fa' ye! -
"Twas wise, tho' fools may ca't no' brave,
To rin or e'er they saw ye." -
"Aye wife, that's true without dispute,
But lest saunts fail in Zion,
I'll hae to swear *** forc'd me out;
Better he swing than I, on
                              Some hangin' day."

My story's done, an' to be free,
Owre sair, I doubt, they smarted,
Wha wad hae bell'd the cat awee,
Had they no been deserted:
Thae warks pat skill, tho' in my min'
That ne'er was in't before, mon,
In tryin' times, maist folk, you'll fin',
Will act like Donegore men
                              On onie day.